FROM GENERATION TO GENERATION

A TEMPLE EMANU-EL COOKBOOK
Birmingham, Alabama

This cookbook is a collection of favorite recipes, which are not necessarily original recipes.

FROM GENERATION TO GENERATION
A Temple Emanu-El Cookbook

Copyright 2003
Temple Emanu-El
2100 Highland Avenue
Birmingham, AL 35205
205-933-8037 Phone
205-933-8099 Fax
www.ourtemple.org

Library of Congress Number: 2002092140
ISBN: 0-9720769-0-5

Edited, Designed and Manufactured by
Favorite Recipes® Press

FRP

P.O. Box 305142
Nashville, Tennessee 37230
800-358-0560

Book Design: Whitfield Art Agency, Susan Breining
Art Director: Steve Newman
Project Editor: Ginger Dawson

Manufactured in the United States of America
First Printing: 2003
7,500 copies

ACKNOWLEDGMENTS

To our husbands, Dr. Mark Cohen and Dr. Allan Goldstein, for their love and support;
Susan K. Biedinger and Sallie D. Downs for their tireless efforts on behalf of this project;
Jann Blitz for her guidance and time; Dan Monroe and Pinkie Chace for their
friendship and their creative talents; Dr. Lester Seigel for his knowledge and
love of Temple Emanu-El; and to Bob Moody for his generosity.
Lynne Cohen, exterior architectural detail photography

Mark and Lynne Cohen, Sherron and Allan Goldstein,
Cookbook Chairs

CONTENTS

INTRODUCTION

Cooking, sharing, and eating are as woven into our spiritual lives as the complex knot of challah bread. Food is the yeast of memories — memories of past gatherings born on the smells from our kitchens, reveries that drift upon us on the taste of some long forgotten sweet, remembrances of loved ones long passed in fleeting flavors. The simple smells of certain foods conjure whole vistas, long diversions, memories of things past. More importantly, we pass on the memories of our faith with the things we eat together. With some foods we try — we try so very hard- to remember what it must have been like crossing unforgiving lands centuries ago. With others we seek to experience the joys and bitterness of the ages simultaneously. With still others we appreciate the miracle of that little bit of oil. And so food embodies the memories of our culture just as it embodies the memories of our families.

Herein, are recipes that embody the memories of a temple, a temple built almost a hundred years ago with the words, "My house shall be a house of prayer for all people" engraved on its sides. A temple built by families, brought together in faith, love and mutual respect, who have celebrated joys and shared bitterness together. Families who have been a source of strength and a passing forward of tradition and remembrance. Nothing better expresses the strength of our families than their memories.

Every meal begins with a blessing. Our Temple Emanu-El Cookbook is an offering of love . . .
an offering of foods shared with others. Foods prepared with tradition and honor.
Foods lovingly passed down from generation to generation —l'dor l'vor
BLESSING — MOTZI

ברוך אתה יי אלהינו מלך העולם הזן את הכל

Ba-ruch a-ta Adonai, Eh-lo-hei-nu meh-lech ha-o-lam,
Ha-zan et ha-kol
We praise You, Eternal God, Sovereign of the universe;
Who sustains the world with goodness.

Temple Emanu-El is the principal spiritual center for Reform Jews and their families in the greater Birmingham area. We offer to our families a wide range of worship and learning experiences and a warm environment in which to share and support one another in celebration, in healing, and in religious observance. Our congregation provides us many opportunities to engage in action and advocacy projects which encourage social justice, peace, and freedom for all.

Temple Emanu-El was founded in 1882 by early Jewish settlers who came to the small town of Birmingham. By 1886, the Temple's membership had grown to 86 families, and the congregation laid the cornerstone for the first synagogue to be built in Jefferson County. The first house of worship, located on the southeast corner of Fifth Avenue and 17th Street North, served the congregation for the next 24 years. These early settlers assumed leadership roles in all aspects of civic affairs beginning a tradition of community involvement that continues among our Temple membership today.

In 1895, Rabbi Morris Newfield, a young Hungarian immigrant, was elected to lead the congregation—which he continued to do for over 45 years. Under his leadership, the congregation swelled to over 300 families and a "new" sanctuary was built in 1914 at 2100 Highland Avenue. It is this majestic and beautiful sanctuary that we still worship in today. Arriving the day after the attack on Pearl Harbor, Rabbi Milton Grafman took the reins of Temple Emanu-El and led our congregation for the next 34 years—through World War II, the establishment of Israel, and the struggle for civil rights in Birmingham. Thanks to the supreme efforts of both Rabbi Newfield and Rabbi Grafman, Temple Emanu-El has played a vital role in the history and life of Birmingham's Jewish and secular community.

Today, the congregation is led by Rabbi Jonathan Miller, who joined our Temple in 1991. Under his enthusiastic leadership, our congregation continues to grow and flourish in both numbers and activity. He embraces our philosophy of community and is extraordinarily innovative in his programming. Rabbi Miller is joined on the pulpit and in pastoral functions by Cantor Jessica Roskin, a spirited Jewish leader and wonderful musician, and by Rabbi Scott Hausman-Weiss. Rabbi Hausman-Weiss has the unique mission to provide enticing adult educational opportunities to help our congregants discover new ways to connect to their spiritual heritage, the Temple, and the greater Jewish community.

Throughout Temple Emanu-El's history, supportive families have formed a culture of tolerance, love and community. Over the years, Temple has opened its doors to families of all denominations—frequently serving as a place of worship for congregations in need of space. Temple has always been a place of comfort, togetherness, and spiritual wholeness for its congregation. As the inscription on the outside walls of our synagogue says, Temple Emanu-El has always been "a house of prayer for all people."

Consider this cookbook a welcoming to our house, to the tables of our families—a passing on of the rich heritage that is Temple Emanu-El.

Appetizers

VEGETABLE ANTIPASTO

1 cup olive oil
4 garlic cloves, chopped
4 ribs celery, cut into 1-inch pieces
1 pound fresh mushrooms, halved
12 small white onions, quartered
12 ounces pole beans, broken into
*   1-inch pieces*
4 carrots, cut into 1-inch pieces
1 head cauliflower, cut into
*   bite-size pieces*
2 green bell peppers, cut into strips
1 medium eggplant, cubed
12 large pitted green olives
12 large pitted black olives

3 bay leaves
Seasoned salt to taste
Garlic salt to taste
Dried oregano to taste
Dried basil to taste
Dried thyme to taste
Ground pepper to taste
12 slices pimento
2 (2-ounce) cans flat anchovies
1 1/2 cups ketchup
1 cup wine vinegar
2 tablespoons sugar
1 tablespoon prepared yellow
*   mustard*

Heat the olive oil in a Dutch oven over medium-high heat. Add the garlic and sauté until tender. Stir in the celery, mushrooms, onions, beans, carrots, cauliflower, bell peppers, eggplant, green olives, black olives and bay leaves. Season generously with seasoned salt, garlic salt, oregano, basil, thyme and ground pepper.

Cook until the vegetables are tender. Stir in the pimento and undrained anchovies. Combine the ketchup, vinegar, sugar and prepared mustard in a small bowl; mix well. Stir into the vegetable mixture. Season generously with seasoned salt, garlic salt, oregano, basil, thyme and ground pepper. Cook for 5 minutes, stirring frequently. Add additional seasonings, if desired. Remove from the heat and let cool. Chill, covered, overnight. Serve with crusty French bread.

Yield: 8 servings
SANDRA SHULMAN

CAPONATA

1 medium eggplant, sliced	1 (6-ounce) can tomato paste
Kosher salt to taste	2 tablespoons wine vinegar
5 tablespoons olive oil	Celery salt to taste
1 large onion, coarsely chopped	Capers to taste
1 1/2 cups chopped fresh mushrooms	1 (or more) garlic clove, minced

Sprinkle the eggplant slices with kosher salt. Let stand until the eggplant renders juices; drain. Cut the eggplant slices into bite-size pieces. Heat the olive oil in a skillet over medium-high heat. Sauté the eggplant, onion and mushrooms in the hot oil until tender. Reduce the heat and stir in the tomato paste, vinegar, celery salt, capers and garlic. Simmer for 25 minutes, stirring occasionally. Remove from the heat and let cool. Chill, covered, until serving time. Serve with small pieces of challah.

Yield: 6 to 8 servings

JIMMIE HESS

DEVILED EGGS FROM BEA'S KITCHEN

8 hard-cooked eggs	1 1/2 teaspoons vinegar
3 ounces cream cheese, softened	1/2 teaspoon salt
2 to 3 tablespoons mayonnaise	Dash of cayenne pepper
1 1/2 tablespoons dry mustard	

Slice the hard-cooked eggs in half lengthwise. Remove the yolks and press through a sieve into a mixing bowl. Beat in the cream cheese until smooth. Add the mayonnaise, dry mustard, vinegar, salt and cayenne pepper. Mix until smooth. Spoon into the egg whites. You may also spoon into a pastry bag and pipe into the egg whites. Garnish with sliced pimento-stuffed green olives.

Yield: 4 servings

LYNNE AND MARK COHEN

EASY TURKISH FETA PASTRIES

8 ounces feta cheese
1 egg
2 tablespoons chopped fresh dill
1 package frozen puff pastry, thawed

2 tablespoons milk
Black cumin seeds, sesame seeds or
   poppy seeds (optional)

Soak the feta cheese in a bowl of cold water for 30 minutes. Drain and pat dry. Combine the feta cheese, egg and dill in a food processor and process until smooth. Cut the puff pastry into 9 squares per sheet. Top each square with a spoonful of the cheese mixture. Fold the edges of the puff pastry in half to form triangles. Squeeze or press with a fork to seal. Brush the triangles with the milk. Sprinkle with cumin seeds, sesame seeds or poppy seeds. Arrange on a baking sheet. Bake at 425 degrees until golden brown. Serve warm or cold as an appetizer or light lunch.

Yield: 18 appetizer servings
KATIE ICIMSOY

After living in Turkey for a few years, we moved back to the USA. My husband was homesick for foods from his native country, so I learned how to adapt many Turkish recipes to use products available here, and also ways to cut down on the preparation time (as any mother of 2 children under 5 would!). My husband loves these pastries and they disappear in an instant whenever I make them for parties and picnics!

BAKED SALAMI

2 pounds salami, outer covering and
  red paper lining removed
1 bottle chili sauce

1/2 cup packed brown sugar
Worcestershire sauce to taste
2 tablespoons spicy brown mustard

Cut off both ends of the salami. Place on a foil-lined baking sheet, folding the foil around the salami. Combine the chili sauce, brown sugar and Worcestershire sauce in a bowl and mix well. Bake the prepared salami at 275 to 300 degrees for 3 hours, basting with the chili sauce mixture every 30 minutes. Cut the salami into slices and serve with the spicy brown mustard and wooden picks.

Yield: 12 to 16 servings
LETTY MARCUS

CREAM HERRING

3/4 cup mayonnaise
3/4 cup cream
1 teaspoon sugar
1 teaspoon French mustard

1 (16-ounce) bottle herring pieces in
  wine sauce, drained, onions
  discarded
1 onion, thinly sliced

Mix the mayonnaise, cream, sugar and French mustard in a medium bowl. Stir in the herring and onion. Cover and chill.

Yield: 12 servings
SANDRA VINIK

HERRING

1 (16-ounce) bottle herring pieces in
    wine sauce, drained, onions
    discarded
1 large orange, halved
1 lemon, halved

1 large Bermuda or white onion,
    thinly sliced
1 cup sour cream
1 tablespoon wine vinegar

Place the herring in a medium bowl. Slice half the orange and half the lemon as thinly as possible and add to the herring. Squeeze the juice from the remaining orange and lemon halves and add the juice to the bowl. Add the onion, sour cream and vinegar and fold gently to mix. Cover and chill overnight. Serve with thin slices of rye bread or crackers.

Yield: 12 servings
JANE BLUESTEIN

GRAVLAX

1 (3- to 3 1/2-pound) salmon, scaled,
    split into 2 fillets, boned
1 bunch fresh dill
1/4 cup kosher salt

1/4 cup sugar
2 tablespoons black peppercorns,
    crushed

Place one of the fillets, skin side down, in a deep glass, enamel or stainless steel baking dish or loaf pan. Arrange the dill on top. Mix the salt, sugar and peppercorns in a small bowl. Sprinkle on top of the dill. Top with the remaining fillet, skin side up. Cover the fillets with plastic wrap and foil. Top with weights such as covered bricks or cans of food. Chill for 2 to 3 days, turning every 12 hours and basting with the accumulated juices. Scrape off the seasonings and remove to a cutting board, skin side down. Slice very thinly and serve.

    Note: Crush peppercorns by wrapping in a dishcloth and hitting with a rolling pin or use a mortar and pestle.

Yield: 10 servings
CANTOR JESSICA ROSKIN

SMOKED SALMON AND DILL QUESADILLAS

24 (10-inch) flour tortillas
8 cups each shredded Monterey Jack
   cheese and shredded white
   Cheddar cheese
1 cup chopped red onion
1 cup chopped fresh dill
1 cup chopped fresh Italian parsley

2 cups sour cream
1 cup chopped fresh dill
Salt and pepper to taste
1 pound smoked nova salmon, sliced
Chopped fresh dill for garnish
1 (2-ounce) jar black caviar
1 (4-ounce) jar small capers, drained

Place one tortilla on a square of foil. Top with some of the Monterey Jack and Cheddar cheese. Sprinkle with some of the onion, some of the 1 cup dill and parsley. Top with another tortilla and repeat ingredients. Cover with a third tortilla. Wrap in the foil to seal. Repeat with remaining tortillas, Monterey Jack cheese, Cheddar cheese, onion, dill and parsley. Bake at 450 degrees for 10 to 12 minutes. Unwrap and cut into at least 8 wedges. Arrange on a serving platter. Mix the sour cream and 1 cup chopped dill in a bowl. Season with salt and pepper. Spoon a dollop on top of each tortilla wedge. Place a curled slice of the smoked salmon on top of the sour cream. Sprinkle with chopped dill. Spoon a small portion of the caviar on each wedge and sprinkle with the capers. Serve warm or at room temperature.

Yield: 20 servings
SHERRON GOLDSTEIN

CHEESE STRAWS

1 pound sharp or extra sharp
   Cheddar cheese, shredded
3/4 cup (1 1/2 sticks) margarine,
   softened

2 cups all-purpose flour
1 teaspoon salt
1/4 teaspoon cayenne pepper

Beat the Cheddar cheese and margarine in a mixing bowl until well blended. Mix the flour, salt and cayenne pepper in a small bowl. Combine the flour mixture and cheese mixture; beat well. Spoon the dough into a cookie press fitted with a star tip. Press onto an ungreased baking sheet. Bake at 325 degrees for 7 minutes or until lightly browned.

Yield: (about) 4 dozen
GAIL HERMAN
BEA COHEN

VEGGIE PIZZA

2 (8-count) cans refrigerated
   crescent rolls
16 ounces cream cheese, softened
2/3 cup mayonnaise
1 1/2 teaspoons dried dill

Garlic powder to taste
Bite-size pieces of raw vegetables,
   such as broccoli, carrots, bell
   pepper and cauliflower

Unroll the crescent roll dough on an ungreased baking sheet. Press the seams to seal. Bake according to package directions. Let cool on the baking sheet. Beat the cream cheese, mayonnaise and dill in a mixing bowl. Season with garlic powder. Spread on the cooled crust. Top with assorted vegetables and press lightly. Cut into squares and serve.

Yield: 12 servings
GINGER HELD

TORTILLA ROLL-UPS

8 ounces cream cheese, softened
1 cup sour cream
1 (4 1/2-ounce) can chopped green
   chiles, drained
1 (2 1/4-ounce) can chopped black
   olives, drained

1 bunch green onions, chopped
1 (1 1/4-ounce) envelope taco
   seasoning mix
1 (12 1/2-ounce) package large flour
   tortillas

Combine the cream cheese, sour cream, green chiles, black olives, green onions and taco seasoning mix in a bowl; mix well. Spread on the tortillas and roll up. Slice into spirals and serve.

Yield: 12 servings
ALLISON WEIL

GUACAMOLE

2 to 3 avocados, pitted, peeled,
   mashed
3 to 4 plum tomatoes, seeded,
   chopped
1/2 small onion, chopped
2 serrano chiles, seeded, chopped

1 (41/2-ounce) can chopped green
   chiles, drained
1/4 cup chopped fresh cilantro
Juice of 1 lime
Salt and pepper to taste

Stir the avocados, tomatoes, onion, serrano chiles, green chiles, cilantro and lime juice in a bowl until well mixed. Season with salt and pepper. Chill, covered, until serving time.

Yield: (about) 2 cups
KAREN ALLEN

HOT ARTICHOKE DIP

2 (14-ounce) cans quartered
   artichoke hearts, drained well,
   chopped
1/2 cup mayonnaise

1 cup freshly grated Parmesan cheese
Garlic salt to taste
Paprika (optional)

Mix the artichokes, mayonnaise and Parmesan cheese in a bowl until well blended. Season with garlic salt. Spread in a shallow baking dish and sprinkle with paprika. Bake at 350 degrees for 30 minutes. Serve hot with crackers or corn chips.

Yield: (about) 3 cups
BARBARA DEE WEISBERG
BARBARA ALAND

JACK'S FAMOUS HUMMUS

4 garlic cloves
1 teaspoon salt
2 (19-ounce) cans chick-peas, rinsed,
  drained
2/3 cup well stirred tahini
1/4 cup fresh lemon juice

1/4 cup olive oil
1/2 cup water
2 (12-ounce) packages thin pita
  bread
Olive oil

Purée the garlic in a food processor. Add the salt, chick-peas, tahini, lemon juice, 1/4 cup olive oil and water. Process until smooth, stopping to scrape down the sides. Add additional water to thin if desired. Remove to a serving bowl.

Cut each pita with scissors into 8 wedges. Split each wedge at the seam to form 2 triangles. Arrange in a single layer on a baking sheet, rough side up. Brush with olive oil. Bake at 400 degrees for 4 to 10 minutes or until edges are browned. Serve with the hummus.

Yield: 24 servings
BARBARA AND JACK ALAND

EASY THAI SPREAD

16 ounces cream cheese, softened
1 (9-ounce) bottle mango chutney
1/2 cup chopped peanuts

1/2 cup chopped green onions
1/2 cup flaked coconut

Spread the cream cheese in the center of a serving tray. Spread the chutney on top. Sprinkle with the peanuts, then the green onions and top with the coconut. Arrange crackers around the edge and serve.

Yield: 8 servings
JANN BLITZ

HOMEMADE LOW-FAT PIMENTO CHEESE

2 (7-ounce) jars pimentos
2 to 3 (8-ounce) packages shredded
    low-fat cheese, such as Cheddar
    or Mexican mix
Low-fat mayonnaise to taste
Dijon mustard to taste
Prepared yellow mustard to taste

Worcestershire sauce to taste
Tabasco sauce to taste
Garlic powder to taste
Onion powder to taste
Seasoned salt to taste
Dried dill to taste
Salt and pepper to taste

Chop the pimentos, reserving liquid. Mix the pimentos, liquid and cheese in a large bowl. Stir in mayonnaise to the desired consistency. Season with Dijon mustard, prepared yellow mustard, Worcestershire sauce, Tabasco sauce, garlic powder, onion powder, seasoned salt, dill, salt and pepper. Cover and chill to let flavors blend. Best served on rye bread topped with a slice of tomato and broiled until bubbly.

Yield: 15 to 24 servings
CHU-CHI FIERMAN

REUBEN DIP

3 ounces cream cheese
1/4 cup sour cream
1/2 cup shredded Swiss cheese

4 ounces sliced corned beef, finely
    chopped
1/4 cup drained chopped sauerkraut

Combine the cream cheese, sour cream, Swiss cheese, corned beef and sauerkraut in a saucepan. Cook over low heat until hot, stirring occasionally. Thin with milk or sauerkraut juice, if desired. Serve with rye snack sticks.

Yield: 1 1/2 cups
ANNE MICHELSON

Soups

RANDI AND MICHAEL'S BLACK BEAN SOUP

*4 potatoes, peeled, cut into 1- to
  2-inch slices*
*4 (15-ounce) cans black beans,
  rinsed, drained*
1 red bell pepper, chopped
1 green bell pepper, chopped
1 to 2 tomatoes, chopped
1 jalapeño chile, seeded, chopped

1 large onion, chopped
1 tomatillo, chopped
1 (16-ounce) can vegetable broth
3/4 cup (or more) prepared salsa
Cumin, salt and pepper to taste
Shredded Cheddar cheese (optional)
Sour cream (optional)
Prepared salsa (optional)

Cook the potatoes in a large saucepan of boiling water until tender. Drain the liquid. Add the black beans, bell peppers, tomatoes, jalapeño chile, onion, tomatillo, vegetable broth and 3/4 cup salsa. Season with cumin, salt and pepper and mix well. Bring to a boil, reduce the heat to low and simmer for at least 30 minutes. The vegetables should be very soft. Remove from the heat and purée using a hand blender, being careful not to spatter hot soup. Pour into bowls and garnish with Cheddar cheese, sour cream and salsa, if desired.

Yield: 8 servings
LORAINE REZNIK

*Richard Pizitz Family
(left to right): Richard Jr.,
Carrie, Mollie Gotlieb,
Marsha Unger, Rebecca,
Robert Simon, David,
Herman Gotlieb, Andrew.*

FRENCH ONION SOUP

5 tablespoons butter	1/4 teaspoon pepper
1 tablespoon vegetable oil	6 cups beef broth
5 cups sliced yellow onions	1 cup dry sherry
1 teaspoon all-purpose flour	6 slices French bread
1 teaspoon Dijon mustard	1/2 cup shredded Gruyère cheese
1/2 teaspoon salt	6 tablespoons grated Parmesan cheese

Heat the butter and oil in a large saucepan. Add the onions and sauté until well browned. Stir in the flour, Dijon mustard, salt and pepper and cook for 2 minutes. Stir in the broth and sherry. Reduce the heat and simmer for 30 minutes. Divide the soup among 6 heatproof bowls. Top each with a bread slice and sprinkle with the Gruyère cheese and Parmesan cheese. Place under a preheated broiler for 1 to 2 minutes or until the cheese melts and is lightly browned.

Yield: 6 servings
LENORE PICARD

SPLIT PEA SOUP

1 pound green split peas	2 bay leaves
1 large onion, chopped	3 3/4 quarts water
3 large carrots, sliced	Salt and pepper to taste
4 ribs celery, sliced	Chopped fresh parsley
1 1/2 to 2 pounds smoked turkey legs or thighs	

Soak the split peas in enough water to cover in a large saucepan for several hours or overnight. Drain the water from the saucepan. Add the onion, carrots, celery, turkey legs, bay leaves and water. Season with salt and pepper. Cover and bring to a boil. Reduce the heat and simmer for 2 to 3 hours, stirring occasionally. Remove the bay leaves and discard. Remove the turkey legs and remove the meat. Cut into chunks and return to the soup. Add boiling water to the soup if a thinner consistency is desired. Ladle soup into bowls and top with chopped parsley. Serve with boiled noodles or potatoes.

Variation: Add leeks and parsnips for an interesting flavor.

Yield: 12 servings
BETTY STEINMETZ

MUNCY'S SPLIT PEA SOUP

1 pound green split peas
8 cups water
1 chicken bouillon cube
1 large onion, chopped
2 ribs celery, chopped

3 carrots, sliced
Salt and pepper to taste
Garlic powder to taste
Sliced fresh mushrooms to taste
Sherry to taste

Soak the split peas in enough water to cover in a large saucepan for several hours or overnight. Drain the water from the saucepan. Add 8 cups water and bring to a boil. Stir in the bouillon cube, onion, celery and carrots. Season with salt, pepper and garlic powder. Reduce the heat and simmer for 1 hour. Stir in mushrooms. Cook for at least 2 hours, stirring occasionally. Sprinkle with sherry before serving.

Yield: 6 to 8 servings
CATHY MOORE

PUMPKIN MUSHROOM SOUP

1/4 cup (1/2 stick) unsalted butter
1 tablespoon curry powder
1 pound fresh mushrooms, sliced
1 large onion, chopped
1/3 cup all-purpose flour
8 cups chicken stock

2 (16-ounce) cans pumpkin
2 cups heavy cream
3 tablespoons honey
Salt and pepper to taste
Sour cream (optional)

Melt the butter in a stockpot. Add the curry powder. Sauté for 1 minute. Add the mushrooms and onion gradually and sauté until the mushrooms are tender and the onion is translucent. Stir in the flour. Cook for 3 minutes over medium heat. Stir in the stock and pumpkin. Bring to a boil. Reduce the heat and simmer for 20 minutes. Stir in the cream and honey. Simmer for 10 minutes. Season with salt and pepper. Ladle into bowls and top with a dollop of sour cream.

  Variation: Substitute mashed sweet potatoes or yams for the pumpkin for a different flavor. This soup can be made without the mushrooms.

Yield: 8 to 10 servings
CANTOR JESSICA ROSKIN

LAUREN'S MUSHROOM BARLEY SOUP

1/2 cup pearl barley
1 1/2 cups water or stock
3 tablespoons butter
2 garlic cloves, minced
1 (heaping) cup chopped onion
1 pound sliced fresh mushrooms
6 1/2 cups vegetable stock

3 to 4 tablespoons tamari or light
   soy sauce
1/2 teaspoon salt, or to taste
1/2 teaspoon pepper
3 to 4 tablespoons dry sherry
   (optional)

Cover the barley with 1 1/2 cups water in a large saucepan. Cook over medium heat until tender. Melt the butter in a skillet. Add the garlic and onion and sauté until translucent. Add the mushrooms and sauté until tender. Add the mushroom mixture to the barley. Stir in the stock, tamari, salt and pepper. Cover and simmer for 20 minutes. Season with the salt and pepper and stir in the sherry, if desired.

Yield: 6 to 8 servings
BETTY LOEB

Harry Bayer's Soup: Remember, I don't measure everything out. Put in a soup pot of water, sliced mushrooms, barley, the amount determines the consistency, a chopped white onion, chopped carrots, short ribs of beef, garlic salt and pepper. First bring the water to a boil with the short ribs. Then put on simmer and put the barley in. It's a good idea to wash and rinse the barley first. Then gradually put in the other ingredients. Let the soup simmer for several hours, and occasionally stir. I hope this is good enough for you to publish.

THANKSGIVING WEEKEND SOUP

1 (1¹/2-pound) butternut squash
1 tablespoon butter or margarine
2 teaspoons curry powder
1 teaspoon ground cumin
1¹/2 cups coarsely chopped peeled
    Granny Smith apple
    (about 1 large apple)
1 cup finely chopped red onion
1 large garlic clove, minced
3 tablespoons all-purpose flour

3 tablespoons tomato paste
1 cup plain low-fat yogurt
2 (10¹/2-ounce) cans low-sodium
    chicken broth
³/4 teaspoon salt
¹/4 teaspoon freshly ground nutmeg
5 thin slices peeled fresh gingerroot
2 tablespoons dry sherry
¹/4 to ¹/2 cup heavy cream (optional)

Cut the squash in half lengthwise and discard the seeds and membranes. Place the squash cut side down in a shallow baking dish. Add water to a depth of ¹/4 inch. Bake at 400 degrees for 45 minutes or until very tender. (Can be prepared a day in advance.) Let cool and scoop out flesh into a food processor. Process until smooth.

Melt the butter in a large saucepan over medium heat. Add the curry powder and cumin and sauté for 30 seconds. Add the apple, onion and garlic. Sauté for 5 minutes or until tender. Stir in the flour and tomato paste. Add the mashed squash and yogurt and mix well. Add the broth gradually and stir in the salt, nutmeg and gingerroot. Bring to a boil, stirring constantly. Remove from the heat. Stir in the sherry and cream, if desired. Remove the gingerroot and discard.

Note: Pierce slices of gingerroot with a toothpick before adding to the soup for easier removal before serving.

Yield: 6 servings
ELLEN ELSAS

This recipe holds the "most requested by family members" place of honor. It's just the perfect addition to a meal of leftover turkey sandwiches for a Thanksgiving weekend lunch or light supper.

HERBED GAZPACHO

6 cups vegetable juice cocktail
1 cup water
3 beef or vegetable bouillon cubes
1/2 cup red wine vinegar
6 tablespoons olive oil
2 teaspoons Tabasco sauce
2 bunches green onions, trimmed,
    coarsely chopped
1 small orange bell pepper, coarsely
    chopped
2 English cucumbers, seeded,
    coarsely chopped

2 garlic cloves, minced
3 tablespoons fresh thyme leaves
3 tablespoons flat-leaf parsley,
    leaves only
Salt and freshly ground pepper
    to taste
Chopped tomatoes
Chopped cucumbers
Chopped green onions
Seasoned croutons
Sour cream (optional)

Combine the vegetable juice cocktail, water and bouillon cubes in a saucepan. Heat until the bouillon dissolves, stirring occasionally. Add the vinegar, olive oil, and Tabasco sauce and stir to mix. Remove from the heat. Combine the green onions, bell pepper, cucumbers and garlic in a food processor. Add some of the bouillon mixture. Process until the consistency of a chunky broth. Pour into a bowl and stir in the remaining bouillon mixture, thyme and parsley. Season with salt and pepper. Chill, covered, for at least 4 hours. Ladle into soup bowls and let guests garnish with tomatoes, cucumbers, green onions, croutons and sour cream, if desired.

Yield: 6 servings
SHERRON GOLDSTEIN

BLOODY MARY SOUP

5 cups vegetable juice cocktail
1/2 cup vodka
2 tablespoons tomato purée
2 tablespoons Worcestershire sauce
1 tablespoon butter
1 tablespoon sugar
1 tablespoon lemon juice

1/2 teaspoon salt
1/4 teaspoon pepper
1/8 teaspoon onion flakes, or dash of
    onion powder
Dash of dried parsley
Dash of celery seeds
6 lemon or lime slices

Combine the vegetable juice cocktail, vodka, tomato purée, Worcestershire sauce, butter, sugar, lemon juice, salt, pepper, onion flakes, parsley and celery seeds in a saucepan. Heat over low heat until simmering. Ladle into soup bowls and float a slice of lemon on top.

Yield: 6 servings
DIAN DIAMOND

CURRIED ZUCCHINI SOUP

1 tablespoon vegetable oil
1 large onion, chopped
5 medium zucchini, sliced

4 cups (about) vegetable or chicken
    broth
1 1/2 teaspoons curry powder

Heat the oil in a saucepan. Add the onion and sauté until translucent. Add the zucchini and broth and cook until the zucchini is tender. Remove from the heat. Purée in a food processor or blender when cool. Stir in the curry powder. Serve hot or chilled.

Yield: 6 servings
JIMMIE HESS

CABBAGE SOUP

1 onion, chopped
1 (3- to 4-pound) beef chuck roast,
    cut into pieces
8 cups water
2 (28-ounce) cans whole tomatoes

2 (15-ounce) cans tomato sauce
4 (16-ounce) packages shredded
    cabbage
Sugar to taste
Sour salt to taste

Combine the onion, beef and water in a large saucepan. Bring to a boil and cook for 1 1/2 hours. Add the tomatoes and tomato sauce and boil for 1 hour. Stir in the cabbage and cook until the cabbage is soft. Season with sugar and sour salt.

Yield: 10 servings
CISSY HELD

LENTIL SOUP

8 ounces boneless beef chuck, cut
    into pieces
1 soup bone
12 cups water
1 1/2 cups lentils
4 to 5 ribs celery, chopped

3 carrots, sliced
1 onion, chopped
3 garlic cloves, minced
1 1/2 tablespoons salt, or to taste
Sliced kosher knockwurst

Combine the beef, soup bone and water in a large saucepan. Bring to a boil and skim the surface. Add the lentils, celery, carrots, onion, garlic and salt. Reduce the heat and cover. Simmer for 3 hours. Add sliced knockwurst and heat through. Serve with sliced knockwurst in each bowl.

Yield: 10 servings
PHOEBE M. COTTON

This has been a family favorite for four generations. My children and grandchildren were dumbfounded to learn that there are people who have never had lentil soup. My mother always put a pot of lentil soup on to cook when the skies turned gray and the temperature became chilly. The above recipe is for those who prefer a less hardy version; our family likes a thicker soup and I use 1 3/4 cups lentils to suit our palate.

MOM'S VEGETABLE SOUP

16 veal or beef shanks, cut into
    pieces
14 cups water
3 (10³/4-ounce) cans beef broth
3 (14¹/2-ounce) cans stewed
    tomatoes
4 onions, halved
4 ribs celery, sliced
3 to 4 carrots, sliced
¹/4 to ¹/2 cup pearl barley

2 (16-ounce) bags frozen cut okra
2 (16-ounce) bags frozen mixed
    vegetables
5 (1³/4-ounce) envelopes vegetable
    or minestrone soup mix
2 tablespoons sugar
2 teaspoons salt
1 teaspoon pepper
Cavender's all-purpose Greek
    Seasoning to taste

Combine the veal shanks, water, broth, stewed tomatoes, onions, celery, carrots, barley, okra, mixed vegetables, soup mix, sugar, salt and pepper in a large saucepan. Season with Cavender's. Bring to a boil. Reduce the heat and cover. Simmer for 3 to 4 hours.

Yield: 12 servings
JUDY ROTENSTREICH

STAY ABED STEW

Stay Abed Stew is wonderful when you're not feeling up to par but have to see the family anyway. Relax, go shopping, go back to bed, or whatever you please, and in five hours your stew is ready to eat.

2 pounds boneless beef, cut into
    cubes
1 (15-ounce) can baby peas
1 cup sliced carrots
2 potatoes, peeled, sliced
2 ribs celery, chopped

1 (10³/4-ounce) can condensed
    cream of mushroom, tomato or
    celery soup
¹/2 cup water
1 teaspoon salt
Dash of pepper

Mix the beef, peas, carrots, potatoes, celery, soup, water, salt and pepper in a large baking dish and cover with a tight-fitting lid. Bake at 275 degrees for 5 hours.

Yield: 5 to 6 servings
JUDY C. RUTSTEIN

HOMEMADE VEGETABLE SOUP

1 onion, chopped
1 to 1½ pounds ground beef or
   cubed stew beef
1 bunch celery, sliced
1 (46-ounce) bottle vegetable juice
   cocktail
1 (10¾-ounce) can beef broth

1 (10¾-ounce) can condensed
   cream of mushroom soup
1 (16-ounce) package frozen
   vegetable soup mix
½ cup cooking sherry, or to taste
Anne-Katrin's Herb Mix to taste
Uncooked spaghetti

Brown the onion and ground beef in a large Dutch oven. Add the celery and cook until soft. Stir in the vegetable juice cocktail, broth, mushroom soup, frozen vegetables and cooking sherry. Season with Anne-Katrin's Herb Mix. Add uncooked spaghetti as desired. Cook over low heat for 30 to 45 minutes. Even better the second day.

Yield: 4 to 6 servings
ILENE ROSENFELD JOHNSON

SANTA FE SOUP

2 pounds ground beef
2 (1¼-ounce) envelopes taco
   seasoning mix
2 (1-ounce) envelopes ranch salad
   dressing mix
2 (16-ounce) cans each red, pinto
   and black beans

2 (16-ounce) cans undrained white
   kernel corn
1 (16-ounce) can undrained stewed
   tomatoes
1 (16-ounce) can undrained
   tomatoes with green chiles
1 to 2 cups water

Brown the ground beef in a large saucepan. Stir in the taco seasoning mix, salad dressing mix, beans, corn, stewed tomatoes, tomatoes with green chiles and water. Simmer until hot.

Yield: 10 servings
MARILYN TANNER

MeMaw's Chili

1 1/2 pounds ground beef or turkey
1 large onion, chopped
1 garlic clove, minced
Mexene chili powder to taste
2 (16-ounce) cans whole tomatoes, crushed

2 (16-ounce) cans Van Camp's New Orleans style red kidney beans
Salt and pepper to taste
Hot cooked rice

Brown the ground beef, onion and garlic in a large deep cast-iron skillet. Season with Mexene chili powder. Stir in the tomatoes and red beans. Simmer over low heat until flavors blend. Serve over rice.

Yield: 4 to 6 servings
Elaine Kartus
Sallie Datnoff Downs

Chicken Corn Chowder

1 medium chicken, cut up
2 (10 3/4-ounce) cans chicken broth
1 onion, chopped
2 carrots, sliced
3 ribs celery, sliced

1 large potato, peeled, cubed
1 (8-ounce) can tomato sauce
1 cup chopped fresh parsley
2 (15-ounce) cans cream-style corn
2 medium zucchini, sliced

Combine the chicken, broth, onion, carrots, celery, potato, tomato sauce and parsley in a large saucepan or slow cooker. Cook until the vegetables are tender and the chicken is cooked through. Remove the chicken and cut into bite-size pieces, discarding skin and bones. Return to the saucepan. Add the corn and zucchini during the last 15 minutes of cooking.

Yield: 6 servings
Harriet Cogan

RANCH-STYLE CHICKEN SOUP

Broth

16 cups water
1 cup chopped onion
1 1/2 teaspoons salt
1 teaspoon dried marjoram
1 teaspoon dried thyme
6 garlic cloves, sliced
4 to 5 bay leaves
1 (6-pound) roasting chicken

Soup

5 cups chopped seeded plum
   tomatoes
2 cups chopped carrots
10 red potatoes, halved
1 1/2 cups cut green beans
2 teaspoons salt
2 ears fresh corn, cut crosswise into
   1/2-inch pieces
1 cup chopped onion
3/4 cup fresh cilantro, chopped
1/4 to 1/3 cup chopped seeded
   jalapeño chiles
8 lime wedges

For the broth, combine the water, onion, salt, marjoram, thyme, garlic, bay leaves and chicken in a large stockpot. Bring to a boil and reduce the heat. Simmer for 40 minutes or until the chicken is cooked through. Remove the chicken and let cool. Remove the meat from the bones and shred with two forks. Cover and chill the meat. Return the bones to the cooking liquid. Cover partially and simmer for 1 hour. Strain the broth through a sieve into a large bowl. Discard the solids. Cover the broth and chill for 8 hours or overnight. Skim the fat from the broth and discard.

For the soup, bring the broth to a simmer in a large saucepan over medium heat. Add the tomatoes, carrots and potatoes. Cover partially and cook for 25 minutes or until the vegetables are tender. Add the cooked chicken, green beans, salt, corn and onion. Cook for 10 minutes or until heated through. Ladle the soup into 8 bowls. Top each with 1 to 2 tablespoons chopped onion, 1 tablespoon chopped cilantro and 2 teaspoons jalapeño chile. Serve with a lime wedge.

Yield: 8 servings
SHERRON GOLDSTEIN

GRANDMA'S CHICKEN SOUP

12 cups water
Salt to taste
1 (3- to 4-pound) chicken, quartered
1 beef soup bone
2 ribs celery with leaves, coarsely
    chopped
1 small onion, coarsely chopped

2 carrots, cut into quarters
1 parsley sprig
1/8 teaspoon nutmeg
Pepper to taste
Cooked noodles, rice or matzo balls
    to taste

Bring the water to a boil in a large saucepan. Salt the chicken lightly and add carefully to the boiling water. Add the beef soup bone, celery, onion, carrots, parsley and nutmeg when the water returns to a boil. Season with salt and pepper. Reduce the heat and simmer until the chicken is cooked through. Remove the chicken and beef soup bone and let cool. Strain the soup through a sieve into a saucepan and discard the solids. Remove the meat from the bones. Return some or all of the meat to the soup. Add cooked noodles, rice or matzo balls and cook until heated through.

Yield: 8 servings
JULIE MARKS

This recipe by my grandmother, Esther Kahn Marks, originally appeared in a Hadassah cookbook, which was published in Birmingham in the 1950s. My grandmother was a member of Temple Emanu-El when she was a child. During the 1940s and 1950s, she was a well-respected caterer.

ROASTED CHICKEN SOUP

1 medium chicken
Salt and black pepper to taste
1/4 cup (1/2 stick) butter, softened
1 cup finely chopped celery
1 cup finely chopped carrots
1 tablespoon grated onion

2 cups white rice, cooked
2 (10³/4-ounce) cans condensed
*   cream of chicken soup*
2 cups whole milk
Cayenne pepper to taste

Place the chicken on a rack in a roasting pan. Season with salt and black pepper. Bake at 350 degrees for 20 minutes. Spread the surface of the chicken with butter. Bake at 350 degrees until cooked through. Remove to a platter and let cool. Let the drippings cool. Skim the fat from the cooled drippings and reserve. Pour the skimmed liquid into a large saucepan. Cut the chicken into bite-size pieces, discarding skin and bones. Add the chicken, reserved fat, celery, carrots and grated onion to the broth. Simmer over medium heat for 20 minutes. Add the rice, soup, milk, salt, black pepper and cayenne pepper. Simmer for 30 minutes; do not boil. Add canned chicken broth as needed for additional broth.

Yield: 8 servings
PAT SAUL

Salads

CILANTRO LIME VINAIGRETTE

2 tablespoons lime juice
1 garlic clove (or more), minced
1/2 teaspoon sugar
1/2 teaspoon kosher salt

1/8 teaspoon ground coriander
(optional)
2 tablespoons extra-virgin olive oil
1 tablespoon chopped fresh cilantro

Combine the lime juice, garlic, sugar, salt and coriander in a small bowl. Whisk in the olive oil and cilantro. Serve over a buttery lettuce such as Boston, red or green leaf lettuce.

Yield: (about) 1/3 cup
CANTOR JESSICA ROSKIN

FROM GENERATION TO GENERATION SALAD

1 head iceberg lettuce, torn into bite-
size pieces
1 to 2 tomatoes, cut into wedges
1 sweet onion, sliced
1 cucumber, sliced
1 avocado, pitted, peeled, cut into
bite-size pieces

Olive oil to taste
Red wine vinegar to taste
Anchovy paste to taste
Cavender's all-purpose Greek
Seasoning to taste

Combine the lettuce, tomatoes, onion, cucumber and avocado in a large bowl. Whisk olive oil, vinegar and anchovy paste in a small bowl. Season with Cavender's. Add to the salad and toss to coat.

Yield: 4 to 6 servings
JUDY ROTENSTREICH

Nothing fancy but everyone tries to duplicate it. No generation thinks
they make it as good as their mother did. My card game "claims" that's
all they want when it's my turn.

JOANIE BAYER'S CAESAR SALAD

1 (2-ounce) can anchovies, drained,
    mashed
1/3 cup vegetable oil
1/4 cup lemon juice
1 tablespoon Worcestershire sauce
1/2 teaspoon salt
1/2 teaspoon pepper
1/4 teaspoon dry mustard

1 garlic clove, crushed (optional)
2 eggs
1 head romaine, torn into bite-size
    pieces
Freshly grated Parmesan cheese
    to taste
Croutons to taste

Whisk the anchovies, oil, lemon juice, Worcestershire sauce, salt, pepper, dry mustard and garlic in a small bowl. Bring a saucepan of water to a boil. Remove from the heat and break the eggs into the hot water. Cook for 1 1/2 minutes. Remove with a slotted spoon and whisk into the dressing. Toss the lettuce, cheese, croutons and dressing in a large bowl. Serve immediately.

Yield: 4 servings
GAIL AND JEFFREY BAYER

CHARLES' CAESAR DRESSING

4 garlic cloves, crushed
6 anchovies, mashed
1/4 cup olive oil
Juice of 2 lemons
1 tablespoon Worcestershire sauce
1/2 teaspoon salt

1/4 teaspoon dry mustard
Few dashes Tabasco sauce
1 egg
1/2 cup freshly grated Parmesan
    cheese

Mix the garlic, anchovies, olive oil, lemon juice, Worcestershire sauce, salt, dry mustard and Tabasco sauce in a small bowl. Whisk in the egg and cheese.

    Note: To avoid raw eggs that may carry salmonella, we suggest using an equivalent amount of pasteurized egg substitute.

Yield: (about) 1 1/2 cups
KIM ROSEMORE

BROCCOLI SALAD

1/4 cup (1/2 stick) butter or
    margarine
1 (3-ounce) package ramen noodles,
    crushed
1/2 to 1 cup chopped walnuts
1 bunch red leaf or mixed lettuces

1 crown broccoli, cut into florets
5 green onions, chopped
1 cup vegetable oil
1/2 cup sugar
1/2 cup white vinegar
2 teaspoons soy sauce

Melt the butter in a saucepan. Add the crushed noodles and walnuts. Sauté until noodles are soft. Remove to paper towels to cool. Combine the lettuce, broccoli, green onions and cooled noodle mixture in a large bowl. Cover and chill until ready to serve. Combine the oil, sugar, vinegar and soy sauce in a jar with a tight-fitting lid. Shake until well mixed. Add to the salad and toss to coat.

Yield: 8 servings
JANE SEIGEL

HEALTHY COLESLAW

1/2 cup white vinegar
1/2 cup water
1/4 cup rice vinegar
2 tablespoons canola oil
1 tablespoon sugar

1 teaspoon celery seeds
Pepper, paprika and dried parsley
    to taste
1 large head cabbage, shredded
4 carrots, shredded

Combine the white vinegar, water, rice vinegar, canola oil, sugar and celery seeds in a saucepan. Season with pepper, paprika and parsley. Bring to a boil and remove from the heat. Combine the cabbage and carrots in a large bowl. Add the hot dressing and toss to coat. Chill, covered, for 24 hours.

Yield: 8 servings
LEONA CHERNER

MARINATED SLAW

1 head cabbage, shredded
   (about 9 cups)
1 large green bell pepper, chopped
1 onion, finely chopped
1 rib celery, chopped
1 1/2 cups sugar

1 cup cider vinegar
1 cup vegetable oil
1 tablespoon salt
1 tablespoon sugar
1 tablespoon chopped pimento

Mix the cabbage, bell pepper, onion and celery in a large bowl. Add 1 1/2 cups sugar and toss to coat. Combine the vinegar, oil, salt and 1 tablespoon sugar in a saucepan. Bring to a boil, stirring constantly. Pour over the cabbage mixture. Add the pimento and toss to coat. Let cool. Chill, covered, until serving time.

Yield: 8 servings
FRANCES G. CYPRESS

MEXICAN SLAW

1 head cabbage, shredded
10 to 12 pitted green olives, sliced
1/2 cup white vinegar
1/2 cup vegetable oil
1/2 cup sugar

1 teaspoon salt
1 teaspoon celery salt
1 teaspoon celery seeds
1 teaspoon dry mustard
1/2 teaspoon pepper

Mix the cabbage and olives in a large bowl. Combine the vinegar, oil, sugar, salt, celery salt, celery seeds, dry mustard and pepper in a saucepan. Bring to a boil and boil for 3 minutes. Pour over the cabbage mixture and toss to coat. Chill, covered, until serving time.

Yield: 8 servings
ELLEN DORSKY

ORIENTAL COLESLAW

2 (3-ounce) packages ramen noodles,
    crumbled
1 to 2 (16-ounce) packages angel
    hair slaw
1 cup slivered almonds, toasted

1 cup dry roasted sunflower seeds
1 bunch green onions, sliced
1 cup vegetable oil
1/2 cup sugar
1/3 cup vinegar

Combine the ramen noodles, slaw, almonds, sunflower seeds and green onions in a large bowl. Whisk the oil, sugar, vinegar and ramen seasoning packets in a bowl. Add to the slaw mixture and toss to coat. Chill, covered, overnight. Toss again before serving.

Yield: 12 to 15 servings
LORI WEIL

CORN BREAD SALAD

3 cups (1/2-inch cubes) dry
    corn bread
1 cucumber, seeded, chopped
1 large tomato, seeded, chopped
1/2 cup chopped red bell pepper
1/2 cup chopped yellow bell pepper
1/4 cup finely chopped red onion
1/4 cup thinly sliced green onions
2 garlic cloves, minced

1/4 cup white wine vinegar
1/3 cup extra-virgin olive oil
1 teaspoon coarsely chopped canned
    chipotle chile
1 tablespoon honey
1/4 cup chopped fresh cilantro
Salt and freshly ground pepper
    to taste

Spread the corn bread in a single layer on a baking sheet. Bake at 350 degrees for 20 minutes or until crisp. Let cool. Combine the cucumber, tomato, bell peppers, red onion, green onions and garlic in a large bowl. Toss to mix. Add the corn bread and lightly toss to mix. Whisk the vinegar, olive oil, chipotle chile, honey and cilantro in a bowl. Season with salt and pepper. Pour over the salad and toss to mix. Let stand for 15 minutes before serving.

Yield: 4 servings
SHERRON GOLDSTEIN

SOUTH AFRICAN RICE SALAD

1/2 cup (or more) mayonnaise
2 tablespoons chutney
Curry powder to taste

2 cups rice, cooked, cooled
1/2 cup chopped red bell pepper
2 nectarines, chopped

Mix the mayonnaise and chutney in a small bowl. Season with curry powder. Place the rice in a bowl and add the mayonnaise mixture. Toss to mix and add more mayonnaise, if needed. Add the bell pepper and nectarines and toss again.

Yield: 8 servings
SANDRA VINIK

MARINATED TOMATOES

4 to 6 tomatoes
3/4 cup olive oil
3 tablespoons wine vinegar
1/2 cup chopped fresh parsley
1 tablespoon chopped chives

1 tablespoon capers
1/2 tablespoon grated onion or finely
*   chopped green onions*
Lemon juice, minced garlic, sugar, dill
*   and oregano to taste*

Dip the tomatoes in a saucepan of boiling water for 30 to 60 seconds or until the skins split. Plunge into cold water and slip off the skins. Quarter the tomatoes and place in a bowl. Add the olive oil, vinegar, parsley, chives, capers and onion. Sprinkle with lemon juice, garlic, sugar, dill and oregano. Stir to mix well. Chill, covered, for 24 hours.

Yield: 8 servings
JUDY ABROMS

When I was in grammar school in Brookline, Mass., one of the electives was cooking. I loved it! One day we learned how to can tomatoes. This was very important because everyone had a Victory Garden during World War II, and I was so proud to be able to "Show My Mother" how to can a vegetable. After the war my parents continued to grow tomatoes and one of our favorite recipes was marinating the tomatoes for salad. This recipe is the combination of my mother's recipe and the recipe of Ida Zeidman who was a dear friend when Hal and I moved to Birmingham.

KOSHER PICKLED TOMATOES

10 green tomatoes, halved	4 sprigs fresh dill
4 carrots, quartered lengthwise	4 to 8 hot chiles
4 ribs celery, halved, leaving some	1 part cider vinegar
leaves attached to the top halves	1 part kosher salt
12 garlic cloves	20 parts water

Place the tomato halves in four 1-quart canning jars. Tuck the carrots, celery and garlic into empty spaces. Add 1 sprig of dill and 1 to 2 chiles to each jar. Stir the vinegar, salt and water in a bowl until the salt dissolves. Pour over the vegetables in the jars almost to the top. Cap the jars loosely. Place the jars in a shallow pan and set in a cool dark place for 5 days for "half-done" pickled tomatoes. Store in the refrigerator for up to 1 month.

Yield: 4 quarts

FERNE SEIGEL

I remember eating them first at my Romanian Jewish Grandmother's house at Friday night Shabbat dinner. Her name was Annie Rotenstreich, and she was the founder of Hadassah's Bubbe Club. She taught my mother how to cook "Jewish," as my mother was an orphan. My father loved these very hot (spicy) dishes, and my mother always had these on our dinner table. One is an eggplant relish, and the other is pickled green tomatoes. I remember very well going to the farmer's market to buy the tomatoes. ("You must be careful not to pick the peffy (soft) ones!") And I remember watching my mother and the maid "canning" them ("putting them up") in Mason jars, à la Miss Daisy.

CRANBERRY RELISH

1/2 cup water
1/2 cup sugar
2 oranges, unpeeled, seeded, finely
   chopped

2 apples, unpeeled, cored, finely
   chopped
2 cups fresh cranberries, cleaned

Combine the water and sugar in a saucepan. Bring to a boil. Stir in the oranges and apples and cook for a few minutes. Add the cranberries and cook, stirring often, until the cranberries pop. Remove from the heat and let cool. Chill, covered, until serving time.

Yield: (about) 6 cups
ETHEL ALAND FLEISHER

CRANBERRY MOLD

1 (6-ounce) package cherry gelatin
2 cups boiling water
1 1/2 cups cold water
2 oranges, halved, seeded
1 (12-ounce) bag fresh cranberries

1 (8-ounce) can crushed pineapple,
   drained
2 tablespoons lemon juice
1 cup chopped pecans
Sugar to taste

Stir the gelatin and boiling water in a large bowl until the gelatin dissolves. Stir in the cold water. Combine the oranges and cranberries in a food processor and process until finely chopped. Add the pineapple, lemon juice and pecans and process just until mixed. Season with sugar. Mixture should be a little tart. Add to the gelatin and stir to mix. Pour into a mold. Chill, covered, until set.

Yield: 8 servings
GAYLE LEITMAN

This cranberry mold was given to me by Aunt Frieda Leitman. She and her husband Alex used to always make it for the family every Thanksgiving. They used an old grinder to grind the cranberries and oranges. I've made this mold for our family Thanksgiving now for over 25 years.

LIME GELATIN SALAD

2 (3-ounce) packages lime gelatin
2 cups boiling water
1 envelope unflavored gelatin
2 cups cold water
1 teaspoon white vinegar
3 ounces cream cheese, softened

1 (15-ounce) can pear halves,
   drained, juice reserved
Chopped pecans (optional)
1 (8-ounce) package pitted dates
Sour cream (optional)

Stir the lime gelatin and boiling water in a large bowl until the gelatin dissolves. Stir the unflavored gelatin and cold water in a bowl until the gelatin dissolves. Add to the lime gelatin and stir in the vinegar. Pour into a lightly oiled ring mold. Mix the cream cheese with enough pear juice to moisten in a small bowl. Stir in the pecans. Pack about 1 tablespoon in the center of each pear half.

Set the stuffed pears and dates carefully in the lime gelatin. Chill, covered, for up to 2 days or until firmly set. Run a knife around the edge or set in 1 inch of hot water for 1 minute and invert onto a serving plate. Set a small bowl of sour cream mixed with pear juice in the center of the mold, if desired.

Yield: 6 servings
FAYE FRIEDMAN

STRAWBERRY MOLD

2 (3-ounce) or 1 (6-ounce) package
  strawberry gelatin
1 1/2 cups boiling water
1 1/2 (10-ounce) packages frozen
  sweetened sliced strawberries

1 (8-ounce) can crushed pineapple,
  drained
1/2 cup finely chopped pecans
1 cup sour cream

Stir the gelatin and boiling water in a large bowl until the gelatin dissolves. Add the frozen strawberries and stir to break apart. Stir in the pineapple and pecans. Remove half the mixture to a bowl. Add the sour cream and mix well. Pour the sour cream mixture into a mold and chill until set. Top with the remaining gelatin mixture. Chill, covered, until set. (Reverse the order if using a baking dish or pan instead of a mold.)

Yield: 8 servings
Susan K. Biedinger

INDIVIDUAL FROZEN SALADS

2 cups sour cream
1/2 cup sugar
1/2 teaspoon lemon juice
1 (20-ounce) can crushed pineapple,
  drained

1 (16-ounce) can Bing cherries,
  drained, coarsely chopped
1 cup pecan pieces
1 banana, coarsely chopped

Mix the sour cream, sugar and lemon juice in a large bowl. Stir in the pineapple, cherries, pecans and banana. Spray paper muffin cup liners lightly with nonstick cooking spray and place in muffin tins. Fill liners 3/4 full with fruit mixture. Freeze until hard. Unwrap and let sit at room temperature for about 10 minutes before serving.

Yield: 18 servings
Jane Seigel

Side Dishes

CREOLE BEANS

2 tablespoons butter
1 cup chopped onion
2/3 cup chopped celery
2 cups drained canned tomatoes,
    chopped (liquid reserved)

2 cups drained canned green beans
1 teaspoon salt, or to taste
1/4 teaspoon pepper, or to taste
Chopped green bell pepper to taste
    (optional)

Melt the butter in a saucepan. Add the onion and celery and sauté until translucent. Stir in the tomatoes, beans, salt, pepper and bell pepper. Add some of the reserved liquid, if desired. Cook until heated through.

Yield: 6 servings
JEANNE HAGEDORN

CHEESY CAULIFLOWER

2 tablespoons butter
1 (10³/4-ounce) can condensed
    cream of chicken soup
1 cup shredded sharp Cheddar
    cheese
1/2 cup mayonnaise

1 teaspoon curry powder (optional)
1 head cauliflower, steamed, cooled,
    cut into florets
Italian-style bread crumbs to taste
Paprika to taste

Melt the butter in a saucepan. Stir in the soup, Cheddar cheese, mayonnaise and curry powder. Cook until the cheese melts, stirring often. Place the cauliflower florets in a baking dish. Pour the cheese sauce over the cauliflower. Top with bread crumbs and sprinkle with paprika. Bake at 350 degrees for 30 minutes.

Yield: 6 servings
BABS PERLMAN

CARROT CASSEROLE

1/2 cup mayonnaise
2 tablespoons prepared horseradish
1 teaspoon salt
1/4 teaspoon white pepper

Dash of paprika
1 pound baby carrots, cooked,
    mashed
1/3 cup buttered bread crumbs

Mix the mayonnaise, horseradish, salt, white pepper and paprika in a bowl. Stir in the carrots. Spoon into a baking dish. Sprinkle with the bread crumbs. Bake at 375 degrees for 15 minutes.

Yield: 4 servings
SALLY GOLDSTEIN

CARROT SOUFFLÉ

1 pound carrots, sliced
Salt to taste
1/2 cup (1 stick) butter or margarine,
    melted
3 eggs or 5 egg whites

1/2 to 1 cup sugar
3 tablespoons all-purpose flour
1 teaspoon baking powder
1 teaspoon vanilla extract

Cook the carrots in boiling salted water in a saucepan for 20 minutes or until tender. Drain and place in a blender. Add the butter. Blend until smooth. Add the eggs, sugar, flour, baking powder and vanilla and blend until smooth. Spoon into a 1-quart baking or soufflé dish coated with nonstick cooking spray. Bake at 350 degrees for 45 minutes or until firm and golden brown on top.

Yield: 4 servings
JENIFER ROTENSTREICH

CORN PUDDING

1/2 cup (1 stick) butter
1/2 cup sugar
2 to 3 tablespoons all-purpose flour
1 cup evaporated milk
3 eggs, well beaten
2 1/2 teaspoons baking powder

6 ears fresh corn, cooked, kernels
    removed
1/4 cup sugar
1/2 teaspoon cinnamon
1 tablespoon butter, melted

Heat 1/2 cup butter and 1/2 cup sugar in a saucepan. Stir in the flour and remove from the heat. Add the milk, eggs and baking powder and mix well. Fold in the corn kernels. Spoon into a buttered 1-quart baking dish. Place the baking dish in a pan and add hot water to come halfway up the sides of the baking dish. Bake at 350 degrees for 40 minutes. Mix 1/4 cup sugar, the cinnamon and 1 tablespoon butter in a small bowl. Sprinkle on top of the corn pudding. Bake for 3 minutes longer.

Yield: 4 servings
SANDRA SHULMAN

VIDALIA ONION PIE

1/4 cup (1/2 stick) butter
3 cups coarsely chopped Vidalia
    onions
2 eggs
1/2 cup cream or sour cream

1/2 teaspoon salt
1/2 teaspoon paprika
1 baked (9-inch) pie shell
1/2 cup (or more) grated Parmesan
    cheese

Melt the butter in a saucepan. Add the onions and sauté until translucent. Mix the eggs, cream, salt and paprika in a bowl. Stir in the onions. Pour into the pie shell and sprinkle with the Parmesan cheese. Bake at 400 degrees for 25 to 30 minutes. Remove to a wire rack to cool slightly. Cut into 12 wedges and serve warm.

Yield: 12 servings
JANN BLITZ

ONION TART

1 1/4 cups butter cracker crumbs
1/4 cup (1/2 stick) butter, softened
2 tablespoons butter
4 cups thinly sliced onions
1/4 cup (1/2 stick) butter
1/4 cup all-purpose flour
1 cup hot milk

1/2 cup hot chicken stock
1 egg yolk
1/2 cup sour cream
Salt and pepper to taste
1 1/2 cups shredded Colby longhorn
    cheese

Mix the cracker crumbs and 1/4 cup softened butter in a bowl. Press over the bottom and up the side of a 9-inch pie plate. Melt 2 tablespoons butter in a heavy skillet. Add the onions and sauté until tender. Melt 1/4 cup butter in a large saucepan. Stir in the flour and cook for 1 minute. Remove from the heat and stir in the milk and stock. Return to the heat and cook until thickened, stirring constantly. Beat the egg yolk in a small bowl. Stir in the sour cream. Add to the hot sauce and stir to mix. Season with salt and pepper. Stir in the onions. Pour into the crumb pie shell. Sprinkle the Colby cheese on top. Bake at 350 degrees for 25 to 30 minutes.

Note: Can be frozen before baking.

Yield: 6 to 8 servings
MARGOT MARX

ROSEMARY NEW POTATOES

1/4 cup olive oil
1 tablespoon Dijon mustard
2 garlic cloves
1 1/2 teaspoons paprika

1/4 teaspoon salt
1 tablespoon rosemary leaves, crushed
2 pounds small new red potatoes,
    halved

Combine the olive oil, Dijon mustard, garlic, paprika and salt in a blender or food processor. Process until smooth. Add the rosemary and pulse a few times until mixed. Combine the potatoes and oil mixture in a 9×13-inch baking pan. Toss to coat and spread in a single layer. Bake at 400 degrees for 1 hour or until potatoes are tender and lightly browned, stirring occasionally.

Yield: 4 to 6 servings
KIM ROTH

SPINACH ARTICHOKE CASSEROLE

2 (14-ounce) cans quartered
    artichoke hearts, drained
1 (8-ounce) can water chestnuts,
    drained, chopped
1 cup (2 sticks) butter or margarine,
    melted
16 ounces cream cheese, softened

6 (10-ounce) packages frozen
    chopped spinach, cooked, drained
Garlic powder to taste
Salt to taste
Pepper to taste
Onion powder to taste
Seasoned bread crumbs to taste

Arrange the artichokes in a 9×13-inch baking dish coated with nonstick cooking spray. Top with the water chestnuts. Mix the melted butter and cream cheese in a large bowl. Add the spinach and mix well. Season with garlic powder, salt, pepper and onion powder. Pour over the artichokes and water chestnuts. Bake at 350 degrees for 30 minutes. Sprinkle with seasoned bread crumbs and bake for 15 minutes longer.

Yield: 10 to 12 servings
JANE SEIGEL

SPINACH SOUFFLÉ

8 eggs
1 teaspoon onion powder, or
    1/4 cup instant minced onion
1/2 teaspoon salt
1/2 teaspoon dried dill
1/4 teaspoon pepper
3 cups cottage cheese
2 cups shredded Cheddar cheese

2 (10-ounce) packages frozen
    chopped spinach, thawed,
    drained
1/2 cup bread crumbs
1 (14-ounce) can quartered artichoke
    hearts, drained, chopped
1 (7-ounce) can sliced mushrooms,
    drained (optional)

Beat the eggs, onion powder, salt, dill and pepper in a large bowl. Add the cottage cheese, Cheddar cheese, spinach, bread crumbs, artichokes and mushrooms and mix well. Spoon into a 3-quart baking dish coated with nonstick cooking spray. Chill, covered, overnight. Bake, uncovered, at 325 degrees for 45 minutes or until set. Cover, if getting too brown.

Yield: 8 servings
JUDY LUKS

SQUASH CASSEROLE

2 pounds yellow squash, sliced
1 large onion, chopped
2 teaspoons sugar
1 teaspoon salt
2 to 3 tablespoons butter, melted

1 cup shredded sharp Cheddar
   cheese
4 eggs, beaten
28 butter crackers, crumbled
2 tablespoons butter, cut into pieces

Combine the squash, onion, sugar and salt in a saucepan. Cover with water and bring to a boil. Cook until tender; drain. Mash the squash and onions in a bowl with a fork. Add the melted butter, Cheddar cheese, eggs and crumbled crackers, reserving about 1/4 cup crumbs. Stir to mix well. Spoon the mixture into a buttered 3-quart baking dish. Sprinkle with the reserved cracker crumbs and dot with 2 tablespoons butter. Bake at 350 degrees for 1 hour or until set.

Yield: 6 servings
CAROLE SIMPSON

SQUASH CASSEROLE

3 pounds yellow squash, sliced
1/2 cup chopped onion
1/2 cup fresh bread crumbs
2 eggs
1/4 cup (1/2 stick) butter, softened

1 tablespoon sugar
1 teaspoon salt
1/2 teaspoon pepper
1/4 cup fresh bread crumbs
1/4 cup (1/2 stick) butter, melted

Boil the squash in a small amount of water in a saucepan until tender, drain. Remove to a bowl and mash. Add the onions, 1/2 cup bread crumbs, eggs, 1/4 cup softened butter, sugar, salt and pepper and mix well. Spoon into a buttered 3-quart baking dish. Sprinkle with 1/4 cup bread crumbs and drizzle with 1/4 cup melted butter. Bake at 375 degrees for about 1 hour.

Yield: 6 servings
CARRIE PIZITZ

GREEN TOMATO CASSEROLE

4 to 5 medium green tomatoes,
   cored, sliced
1 to 2 Vidalia onions, sliced
Olive oil

Salt to taste
1/2 cup grated Romano cheese
1/2 cup seasoned bread crumbs
Dash of cayenne pepper

Arrange a layer of tomatoes and onions in a baking dish coated with olive oil. Season with salt. Top with another layer of tomatoes and onions. Sprinkle with the Romano cheese and bread crumbs. Season with salt and cayenne pepper. Bake at 325 degrees for 1 hour.

Yield: 6 servings
KIM ROSEMORE

OLD–FASHIONED MACARONI AND CHEESE

2 cups medium macaroni, cooked
2 cups shredded Cheddar cheese
3 eggs
1 cup milk

1/2 teaspoon salt
1/8 teaspoon pepper
1/2 cup shredded Cheddar cheese
1 tablespoon butter, cut into pieces

Mix the macaroni and 2 cups Cheddar cheese in a bowl. Spoon into a greased 1 1/2-quart baking dish. Beat the eggs in a bowl. Stir in the milk, salt and pepper. Pour over the macaroni. Sprinkle with 1/2 cup Cheddar cheese and dot with the butter. Bake at 350 degrees for 40 minutes.

Yield: 6 servings
BARBARA ALAND

This recipe was originated by Becky Hebert who worked for my family since before I was born until her death in 1989. She told me the recipe as she made it one day with instructions like "use lots of cheese." Whenever I make it I feel that she is watching over me.

GRANDMA'S MACARONI AND CHEESE

The original recipe was called President Reagan's Macaroni and Cheese, but ask any of Anita May's eight grandchildren and they will call it Grandma's Macaroni and Cheese—always a favorite at family get-togethers.

8 ounces macaroni (2 cups), cooked just until tender, drained
1 teaspoon butter, softened
1 egg, beaten
2³/4 cups shredded sharp Cheddar cheese
1 teaspoon salt

1 teaspoon dry mustard
1 tablespoon hot water
1 cup milk
1/4 cup shredded sharp Cheddar cheese

Mix the macaroni, butter and egg in a bowl. Stir in 2³/4 cups Cheddar cheese. Spoon into a greased 2-quart baking dish. Stir the salt, dry mustard and hot water in a small bowl until dissolved. Stir in the milk. Pour over the macaroni. Sprinkle with 1/4 cup Cheddar cheese. Bake at 350 degrees for 45 minutes or until set and the top is crusty.

Note: Can be frozen before baking. Thaw before baking.

Yield: 6 servings
ANN MOLLENGARDEN

QUAJADO

6 eggs, beaten
1/2 cup cottage cheese
2 (10-ounce) packages frozen chopped spinach, thawed, drained

1/2 cup macaroni, cooked, drained
1 cup grated Parmesan or Romano cheese
1 teaspoon salt
1/2 teaspoon baking powder

Mix the eggs and cottage cheese in a bowl. Stir in the spinach, macaroni, Parmesan cheese, salt and baking powder. Spoon into a greased 9×9-inch baking dish. Bake at 400 degrees for 25 minutes or until a wooden pick inserted in the center comes out clean.

Yield: 6 servings
LORI DORSKY
BEA COHEN

CHEESE GRITS

6 cups water
1 1/2 cups regular grits
16 ounces shredded sharp Cheddar
cheese

3 eggs, lightly beaten
1/2 cup (1 stick) margarine
2 teaspoons seasoned salt
1 teaspoon salt

Bring the water to a boil in a saucepan. Add the grits gradually, stirring constantly. Reduce the heat when the grits return to a boil. Cover and cook for 8 minutes, stirring frequently to reduce lumps. Remove from the heat and stir in the Cheddar cheese. Add the eggs, margarine, seasoned salt and salt and mix well. Pour into a greased 3-quart baking dish. Bake at 350 degrees for 1 hour.

Yield: 6 servings
JUSTIN COHEN

MELANIE DILLENBERG'S DELICIOUS RICE

1/2 cup (1 stick) butter, melted
1 (10 1/2-ounce) can condensed
French onion soup
1 (8-ounce) can sliced water
chestnuts, drained, liquid
reserved

1 (8-ounce) can sliced mushrooms,
drained, liquid reserved
1 cup uncooked converted rice

Mix the butter, onion soup, water chestnuts and mushrooms in a bowl. Pour the reserved liquid from the water chestnuts and mushrooms into the empty soup can. Add water to fill to top. Add to the bowl. Stir in the rice. Pour into a baking dish and cover tightly. Bake at 300 degrees for 1 hour or until liquid is absorbed.

Yield: 4 servings
LYNNE AND MARK COHEN

SPINACH AND MUSHROOM RICE MOLD

2 (10¹/₂-ounce) cans chicken
   broth
1¹/₃ cups white rice
¹/₂ cup (1 stick) butter
2 cups sliced fresh mushrooms
¹/₂ cup chopped green onions

1 (10-ounce) package fresh spinach
   leaves, torn into bite-size pieces
¹/₂ teaspoon seasoned salt
¹/₈ teaspoon cayenne pepper
¹/₄ teaspoon nutmeg
2 dashes ground cloves

Bring the broth to a boil in a saucepan. Stir in the rice and reduce the heat. Cover and cook for 25 minutes. Remove from the heat. Melt the butter in a large skillet coated with nonstick cooking spray. Add the mushrooms and green onions and sauté until tender. Add the spinach and cover. Cook for 5 minutes or until the spinach wilts. Stir in the hot cooked rice, seasoned salt, cayenne pepper, nutmeg and cloves and mix well. Pack into a 5-cup mold coated with nonstick cooking spray. Cover with plastic wrap and let stand for 5 minutes. Invert onto a serving platter and serve immediately.

Yield: 8 to 10 servings
SANDRA SHULMAN

HOT FRUIT COMPOTE

1 (12-ounce) package pitted prunes
1 (12-ounce) package dried apricots
2 (11-ounce) cans mandarin
   oranges, drained

1 (20-ounce) can pineapple chunks,
   drained
1 (20-ounce) can cherry pie filling
³/₄ cup dry sherry

Layer the prunes, apricots, oranges, pineapple and cherry pie filling in the order listed in a 12- or 13-inch square baking dish. Pour the sherry over the top. Bake at 350 degrees for 30 minutes.

Yield: 10 servings
BETTY LOEB

PINEAPPLE CASSEROLE

2 (20-ounce) cans pineapple chunks,
    drained, 1/2 cup juice reserved
5 tablespoons all-purpose flour
1/2 cup sugar

2 cups shredded Cheddar cheese
35 butter crackers, crushed
1/2 cup (1 stick) margarine, melted

Layer the pineapple in a 9x13-inch baking dish and top with the reserved pineapple juice. Mix the flour and sugar in a small bowl. Sprinkle over the pineapple. Layer the Cheddar cheese on top. Mix the crushed crackers and melted margarine in a bowl. Sprinkle over the cheese layer. Bake at 350 degrees for 45 to 55 minutes.

Yield: 8 servings
CELESTE FLEISHER

BRANDIED CRANBERRIES

1 pound fresh cranberries
2 cups sugar

1/4 cup brandy
1/4 cup sugar

Layer the cranberries in a shallow baking dish. Sprinkle with 2 cups sugar. Bake, covered, at 350 degrees for 1 hour. Sprinkle with the brandy and 1/4 cup sugar. Let cool. Chill, covered, for up to 3 weeks.

Yield: (about) 2 1/2 cups
KIT ROTH AND JOANIE BLACH

ROMANIAN RELISH

1 eggplant
2 green bell peppers, halved, seeded
1 red bell pepper, halved, seeded
1 onion, finely chopped

Olive oil to taste
Salt and pepper to taste
Tabasco sauce to taste
Lemon juice to taste

Pierce the eggplant with a fork and place on a baking sheet. Bake at 400 degrees for 1 hour. Remove to a wire rack to cool. Peel and coarsely chop and place in a bowl. Arrange the bell peppers, cut side down, on a baking sheet. Place under the broiler close to the heat source. Broil until the skins turn dark brown, not black. Remove to a paper bag. Close the bag and let stand for 20 minutes. Peel and coarsely chop and add to the eggplant. Add the onion and a small amount of olive oil. Season with salt and pepper. Mix gently. Sprinkle with Tabasco sauce and lemon juice.

Note: Substitute 4 roasted, chopped, hot chiles for the Tabasco sauce for a hotter relish.

Yield: 4 servings
FERNE SEIGEL

SPECIAL FORMULA DILL PICKLES

1 bunch fresh dill
1/4 cup mixed pickling spices
10 to 20 medium pickling
    cucumbers

12 large garlic cloves
8 cups water
1/2 cup white vinegar
6 tablespoons pickling salt

Arrange half the dill and half the mixed pickling spices in the bottom of a 2-gallon crock. Add the cucumbers and garlic in alternating layers. Top with the remaining dill and mixed pickling spices. Stir the water, vinegar and pickling salt in a bowl until the salt dissolves. Pour over the cucumbers in the crock. Set a plate on top, weighted with bags or jars of water, to keep the cucumbers submerged. Let stand at room temperature for 4 to 5 days. Remove the pickles to canning jars and fill with the brine solution. Store in the refrigerator for up to 1 month.

Yield: 10 to 20 pickles
ADELINE F. KAHN

Main Dishes

LEAN AND EASY ROAST BEEF

1 (4- to 5-pound) eye-of-round beef
  roast
5 garlic cloves, slivered
Worcestershire sauce to taste
Lemon pepper to taste

1/2 cup red wine
1/2 cup beef broth
1 teaspoon Kitchen Bouquet
  (optional)

Set the roast on a work surface. Insert the garlic slivers into the fat side of the roast. Season thoroughly with Worcestershire sauce and lemon pepper. Let roast stand until it reaches room temperature. Place the roast fat side up on a rack in a roasting pan. Roast at 450 degrees for 20 minutes. Reduce the heat to 325 degrees and roast for 45 minutes or until done to taste. Remove the roast to a slicing board and let stand for 5 to 10 minutes. Add the wine and broth to the roasting pan. Cook, stirring constantly, over medium heat until boiling. Add the Kitchen Bouquet for color. Cut the roast diagonally into very thin slices. Serve with the gravy, a rice pilaf and a tossed green salad.

Yield: 8 servings
FERNE SEIGEL

PRIME RIB

Sonia "Sunny" Rosen Lazarus cooked this for many Sabbath meals. The dinner table included Ida and Dave Rosen, Celia Sherry, Sunny and Marvin Lazarus and their children, Steve and Nancy. The tradition continues with Steve's children Jes, Tracy, and Mary Alice, and Nancy's children Brad, Josh, and Shannon—four generations at Temple Emanu-El!

1 large bone-in prime rib roast   Prepared mustard to taste

Coat the sides of the roast generously with prepared mustard. Place on a rack in a roasting pan. Roast at 325 degrees for 23 minutes per pound for rare, 27 minutes per pound for medium or 32 minutes per pound for well-done beef.

Yield: 8 to 10 servings
NANCY DENNEY

BARBECUED BRISKET

1 (5- to 7-pound) beef brisket	2 teaspoons prepared mustard
Salt to taste	3/4 cup water
Garlic salt to taste	6 tablespoons Worcestershire sauce
Pepper to taste	6 tablespoons (or less) brown sugar
1 (14-ounce) bottle ketchup	1 cup chopped celery

Season the brisket with salt, garlic salt and pepper. Place on a rack in a dry roasting pan. Roast at 325 degrees for several hours or until tender. Reserve 1/2 cup pan drippings and remove the brisket to a cutting board. Stir the ketchup, prepared mustard, water, Worcestershire sauce, brown sugar, celery and reserved drippings in a saucepan. Bring to a simmer and cook for 1 hour. Slice the cooked brisket and arrange in a shallow pan. Cover with the sauce. Chill, covered, for 24 hours. Bake, covered, at 300 degrees for 1 hour. Serve with cooked potatoes or chill and reheat and serve on bread as sandwiches.

Yield: 8 to 10 servings
DONNA GOLDBERG

HUNGARIAN GOULASH

This recipe was given to me by my friend Ruth Van Wezel about fifty years ago. It was passed down to her from her family in Hungary.

1/4 cup vegetable oil	1 cup water
2 large onions, chopped	1 teaspoon each salt and paprika
1 to 2 tablespoons all-purpose flour	1 1/2 teaspoons pepper
2 pounds beef chuck, cubed	5 medium potatoes, peeled (optional)
1 beef soup bone	1 tablespoon caraway seeds
1/2 cup canned tomatoes	Hot cooked noodles (optional)

Heat the oil in a large saucepan. Add the onions and sauté until translucent. Remove with a slotted spoon to a bowl. Sprinkle the flour over the beef cubes in a bowl. Add to the hot oil along with the soup bone. Cook until browned. Stir in the onions, tomatoes, water, salt, paprika and pepper. Cover and reduce the heat. Cook for at least 1 hour. Add the potatoes and additional water, if needed. Cook until the potatoes are tender. Stir in the caraway seeds. Serve over hot cooked noodles if made without potatoes.

Yield: 4 to 6 servings
ESTHER GLICK

NONA'S RISOTTO WITH BEEF TIPS

1 tablespoon olive oil
1 pound beef tips
Salt and pepper to taste
Garlic to taste
3 (14-ounce) cans chicken broth
16 ounces white rice

1 (6-ounce) can tomato paste with
*   Italian seasonings*
2 (14-ounce) cans chicken broth
1 teaspoon cinnamon
1/2 cup (or more) grated Parmesan
*   cheese*

Heat the olive oil in a large saucepan. Add the beef tips and season with salt, pepper and garlic. Sauté until browned. Add 3 cans broth and the rice. Stir in the tomato paste. Cook over medium heat, gradually adding 2 cans broth and stirring constantly, for 45 minutes or until the rice is tender, the liquid is absorbed and the texture is creamy. Stir in the cinnamon and Parmesan cheese. Serve with additional Parmesan cheese, if desired.

Yield: 6 servings
JOCELYN MCCLELLAND TANDET

SUPER SHORT RIBS

1 tablespoon olive oil
4 1/2 pounds beef short ribs
2 onions, quartered
1 (8 1/4-ounce) can pineapple chunks
*   in heavy syrup*

1 (14 1/2-ounce) can beef broth
1/2 cup chili sauce
1/4 cup honey
3 tablespoons Worcestershire sauce
4 garlic cloves, minced

Heat the olive oil in a Dutch oven over medium-high heat. Add the short ribs and brown well. Stir in the onions, pineapple with syrup, broth, chili sauce, honey, Worcestershire sauce and garlic. Cover and bake at 350 degrees for 1 hour. Uncover and bake for 1 hour longer or until the ribs are very tender.

Yield: 6 servings
MACKIE HOROWITZ

To prepare Betty Loeb's Casino Mustard Sauce, combine 1/4 cup mayonnaise, 1 tablespoon plus 1 1/2 teaspoons Escoffier Sauce, 1 tablespoon plus 1 1/2 teaspoons steak sauce, 1 teaspoon Worcestershire sauce, 2 teaspoons English mustard and 2 teaspoons spicy brown mustard in a small bowl. Serve with beef or chicken. Yield: 1/2 cup

LOW-FAT MEAT LOAF

3 slices wheat bread, torn into pieces
1/4 cup skim milk
1 1/4 pounds lean ground round
1/2 cup egg substitute
1/4 cup ketchup
1/4 cup chopped onion

2 tablespoons chopped fresh parsley,
   or 2 teaspoons dried parsley
1 garlic clove, minced
1/2 teaspoon salt
1/4 teaspoon dry mustard
1/4 teaspoon pepper

Soak the bread in the milk in a bowl for 5 minutes. Add the ground round, egg substitute, ketchup, onion, parsley, garlic, salt, dry mustard and pepper. Stir to mix well. Shape into a loaf and place in a loaf pan. Bake at 350 degrees for 50 to 60 minutes or until cooked through. Cut into 6 slices.

Yield: 6 servings
SHIRLEY LEADER

MEAT LOAF

4 pounds ground round
1 large onion, finely chopped
1 tablespoon salt
1/2 teaspoon pepper
3 eggs
3 garlic cloves, crushed

1 (10 3/4-ounce) can condensed
   tomato soup
1/2 soup can water
1 cup matzo meal
Ketchup to taste

Combine the ground round, onion, salt, pepper, eggs, garlic, soup and water in a bowl. Mix with hands until well combined. Stir in the matzo meal. Shape into 2 loaves and place in loaf pans. Spread ketchup over the top of each loaf. Bake at 375 degrees for 1 1/4 hours or until cooked through.

Yield: 12 servings
MACKIE HOROWITZ

NANA EDITH'S SWEET-AND-SOUR MEATBALLS

2 pounds ground beef	Pepper to taste
2 eggs	2 (8-ounce) cans tomato sauce
2 slices challah	3 to 4 tablespoons grape jelly
Garlic powder to taste	Sugar to taste
Onion powder to taste	Brown sugar to taste
Salt to taste (unless you are using kosher meat)	Lemon juice to taste

Combine the ground beef, eggs and challah in a food processor. Season with garlic powder, onion powder, salt and pepper. Process until well mixed. Form into small balls. Drop into a pot with just enough boiling water to cover the meatballs. Simmer until the meatballs are cooked through. Do not drain. Stir in the tomato sauce and grape jelly. Sprinkle with sugar, brown sugar and lemon juice. Cook until heated through.

Yield: 6 servings
NATALIE HAUSMAN-WEISS

Nana Edith is a fabulous Grandma. She is always interested in her children's and grandchildren's lives and always has an opinion. She seems to thrive on tzurres (trouble). So if there isn't enough already, she's happy to create some! I treasure our regular 5 cents a minute Sunday morning calls that usually begin with, "Hello dolly, did I wake you? Anyway..." I have decided that in an effort to tame the tzurres and kvetching-filled phone conversations, I would probe Nana for her recipes. Her recounting of her recipes has served as an excellent means of communication! Nana doesn't believe in measurements. She shidarines (Yiddish for "a little of this and a little of that") hence the lack of specifics in her recipes.

SWEET-AND-SOUR MEATBALLS

1 pound ground beef
Salt to taste
1/2 cup ketchup
1/2 cup water
3 bay leaves
2 teaspoons Worcestershire sauce

1/4 cup vinegar
Juice of 1/2 lemon
1/4 cup packed brown sugar
Dash of dry mustard
Crushed gingersnap cookies to taste

Form the ground beef into small balls. Cook in a pot of boiling salted water for 20 minutes or until cooked through; drain. Combine the ketchup, water, bay leaves, Worcestershire sauce, vinegar, lemon juice, brown sugar and dry mustard in a saucepan; mix well. Add gingersnap crumbs to taste. Cook over low heat for about 1 hour. Add the meatballs and continue cooking to blend the flavors.

Yield: (about) 20 appetizer meatballs
MITZI KRONENBERG

PORCUPINE MEATBALLS

1 pound ground beef or turkey
1/2 cup uncooked rice
1 teaspoon salt
1/4 teaspoon pepper
2 tablespoons (or more) grated onion

1 cup water
2 to 3 carrots, cut into thin strips
Ketchup to taste
Worcestershire sauce (optional)

Mix the ground beef, rice, salt, pepper and onion in a bowl. Form into balls, handling lightly. Arrange in a skillet with a lid. Pour the water into the skillet and sprinkle with the carrot strips. Top with a generous amount of ketchup. Season with Worcestershire sauce. Cover and bring to a boil over high heat. Reduce the heat and simmer for 1 hour or until cooked through, basting every 15 minutes. Add more water during cooking, if needed.

Yield: 4 servings
ANNE MICHELSON

STUFFED CABBAGE

1 head cabbage
1¹/2 pounds ground chuck
Salt and pepper to taste
1 (5¹/2-ounce) can tomato juice
¹/4 cup vinegar
¹/4 cup corn syrup

Cinnamon to taste
Ginger to taste
Chicken fat
1 green bell pepper, chopped
1 onion, chopped
¹/2 cup water

Core the cabbage and remove the outer leaves. Trim the tough base of the leaves. Blanch the leaves in boiling water for 2 minutes; drain. Season the ground chuck with salt and pepper in a bowl. Place about ¹/4 cup of the ground chuck on a cabbage leaf. Tuck in sides and roll up. Repeat with remaining cabbage leaves and beef. Arrange the stuffed cabbage in a large saucepan. Chop the remaining cabbage and add to the saucepan. Add the tomato juice, vinegar and corn syrup. Season with cinnamon, ginger, salt and pepper. Heat the chicken fat in a skillet. Add the bell pepper and onion and sauté until tender. Add to the stuffed cabbage. Add the water and cover. Simmer for 1¹/2 to 2 hours or until cooked through.

Yield: 8 servings
BETTY GOLDSTEIN

Pat and Leonard Weil

2 pounds ground turkey
2 pounds ground sirloin
Salt and pepper to taste
Seasoned salt to taste
Garlic salt to taste
1 cup chopped onion
4 eggs, beaten
2 heads cabbage, boiled, cooled,
   leaves removed and trimmed

2 to 3 cups drained sauerkraut
2 (28-ounce) cans whole tomatoes,
   partially drained
1/2 cup ketchup
1/2 to 1 cup packed brown sugar
2 to 3 cups water

Mix the ground turkey and ground sirloin in a bowl. Season with salt, pepper, seasoned salt and garlic salt. Add the onion and eggs and mix well. Place about 1/4 cup of the turkey mixture on a cabbage leaf. Tuck in sides and roll up. Repeat with remaining cabbage leaves and turkey mixture. Layer half the sauerkraut in the bottom of a very large saucepan. Arrange half the cabbage rolls in the saucepan. Add the tomatoes, ketchup and brown sugar. Add the remaining cabbage rolls. Top with the remaining sauerkraut and any cabbage not used for making the rolls. Pour the water over all. Cover and bring to a slow boil. Reduce the heat and cook for 2 to 2 1/2 hours or until cooked through. Arrange gently during cooking but do not stir. Add more ketchup and brown sugar if desired.

Yield: 12 to 16 servings
RABBI SCOTT AND NATALIE HAUSMAN-WEISS

SWEET-AND-SOUR ROLLED CABBAGE

1 large head cabbage	1 cup sugar
2 pounds ground beef	3/4 cup lemon juice
1 1/2 cups cornflakes	1 cup water
1 tablespoon salt	1 cup sliced onions, sautéed
1 teaspoon pepper	1 bunch carrots, sliced
1 cup chopped onion	1 cup sliced celery
1 1/2 cups water	1 teaspoon salt
1 (15-ounce) can tomato sauce	1/2 teaspoon pepper
2 (6-ounce) cans tomato paste	6 gingersnaps, crushed

Place the cabbage in the freezer for 30 minutes. Core the cabbage and remove the outer leaves. Trim the tough base of the leaves. Mix the ground beef, cornflakes, 1 tablespoon salt, 1 teaspoon pepper, chopped onion and 1 1/2 cups water in a bowl. Roll into balls and wrap the balls in cabbage leaves. Arrange the stuffed cabbage in a baking dish. Mix the tomato sauce, tomato paste, sugar, lemon juice, 1 cup water, sautéed onions, carrots, celery, 1 teaspoon salt, 1/2 teaspoon pepper and gingersnaps in a bowl. Pour over the cabbage rolls. Bake at 325 degrees for 1 to 1 1/2 hours or until cooked through.

Yield: 8 to 10 servings
NORMA WARREN

STUFFED VEAL BREAST

4 medium potatoes, peeled, grated	Salt and pepper to taste
1 small onion, grated	1 (4- to 5-pound) veal breast,
1 egg, beaten	pocket cut in underside
1 tablespoon all-purpose flour	Paprika to taste

Mix the potatoes, onion, egg and flour in a bowl. Season with salt and pepper. Pack into the pocket in the veal breast. Place in a roasting pan. Season with salt, pepper and paprika. Add a small amount of water to the pan. Roast at 325 degrees until brown and tender or to 160 degrees on a meat thermometer for medium. Turn the meat and baste every 30 minutes during roasting.

Yield: 4 servings
MRS. MILTON (IDA) GRAFMAN

BARBECUE LEG OF LAMB

2 tablespoons olive oil
1 onion, chopped
2 (8-ounce) cans tomato sauce
1 cup water
1/4 cup ketchup
3 tablespoons Worcestershire sauce
2 tablespoons vinegar

1 1/2 teaspoons prepared mustard
Lemon juice to taste
Honey to taste
Hot red pepper sauce to taste
Pepper to taste
1 (2- to 3-pound) boneless leg of
   lamb

Heat the olive oil in a saucepan. Add the onion and sauté until translucent. Stir in the tomato sauce, water, ketchup, Worcestershire sauce, vinegar and prepared mustard. Add lemon juice, honey, hot red pepper sauce and pepper. Simmer for 30 minutes. Place the leg of lamb in a shallow roasting pan. Place under the broiler and brown well on all sides. Remove from the oven. Pour the sauce over the lamb. Bake at 350 degrees for 30 to 45 minutes per pound for medium, basting often.

Yield: 6 to 8 servings
JULIE MARKS

JONATHAN AND CECILY'S ROSEMARY LEMON LAMB CHOPS

5 tablespoons olive oil
4 to 5 garlic cloves, minced
2 tablespoons kosher salt
5 sprigs rosemary, stemmed

Pepper to taste
Juice of 1 lemon
4 lamb chops

Pour the olive oil in a pan large enough to hold 4 lamb chops. Stir in the garlic, salt and rosemary leaves. Season with pepper. Stir in the lemon juice. Add the lamb chops and turn to coat. Let marinate for 10 minutes. Remove the chops and discard the marinade. Grill over high heat for 7 to 10 minutes per side for medium.

Yield: 4 servings
LYNNE AND MARK COHEN

OVEN-ROASTED LEG OF LAMB WITH A POTAGE OF VEGETABLES

1 leg of lamb, boned, butterflied (about 5 pounds)
Several large sprigs of rosemary
2 large bouquet garni (parsley, thyme, rosemary and bay leaf tied in cheesecloth)
4 tablespoons (about) extra-virgin olive oil
Salt to taste

Freshly ground pepper to taste
2 leeks
2 carrots
2 parsnips
2 ribs celery
2 onions, unpeeled, halved
1 bunch flat-leaf parsley
6 large whole garlic bulbs

Open the lamb on a work surface. Arrange 2 sprigs rosemary and 1 bouquet garni down the center. Drizzle with some of the olive oil. Gather the lamb to its original shape and tie with kitchen string. Rub with olive oil and season generously with salt and pepper. Arrange a bed of rosemary sprigs in a roasting pan. Place the lamb on the rosemary. Arrange the leeks, carrots, parsnips, celery, onions, parsley and remaining bouquet garni around the lamb. Trim and discard the top third of each garlic bulb. Place the bulbs, cut side up, around the vegetables and drizzle the garlic with the remaining olive oil. Bake at 425 degrees for 10 to 12 minutes per pound for medium-rare and 15 minutes per pound for medium. Turn the lamb several times during cooking and baste occasionally. Remove the lamb to a cutting board; remove and discard the vegetables. Tent the lamb with foil. Let stand for 25 minutes.

Place the roasting pan over medium heat and scrape up any browned bits. Cook for 2 to 3 minutes, being careful not to burn the drippings. Remove and discard any excess fat. Add several tablespoons of cold water to deglaze the pan. Bring to a boil and simmer for 5 minutes or until thickened. Strain the sauce into a gravy bowl. Carve the lamb into very thin slices and arrange on a warmed serving platter. Surround with the garlic and serve with the gravy.

Yield: 10 servings
SHERRON GOLDSTEIN

To prepare Betty Loeb's Churrasco Sauce, combine 2 cups finely chopped green onions, 1/2 to 1 cup (1 to 2 sticks) butter, 1 cup white wine, 1/4 cup wine vinegar, 1 tablespoon pepper, 1 teaspoon salt and a dash of rosemary in a saucepan. Bring to a boil and cook for 5 minutes. Yield: about 3 cups.

LEG OF LAMB

1 leg of lamb
1 (1-ounce) envelope onion
   soup mix

Seasoned salt to taste
Dale's steak sauce to taste

Trim the fat from the lamb. Place the lamb in a shallow dish and rub with the onion soup mix. Sprinkle with seasoned salt and top with steak sauce. Chill, covered overnight. Remove the lamb and wrap in foil. Grill over indirect heat for 2 to 3 hours or to 160 degrees on a meat thermometer for medium. Turn the meat occasionally during cooking.

Yield: 6 to 10 servings
ROCHELLE KOSLIN

ISRAELI CHICKEN

Dried peaches
Dried apricots
Figs
Raisins

Port
3 (2$1/2$- to 2$3/4$-pound) chickens
Olive oil
Minced garlic

Cook the dried peaches, dried apricots, figs, raisins and a small amount of port in a saucepan for a short time. Remove from the heat and let cool. Rub the cavity and outside of each chicken with olive oil and garlic. Stuff each chicken with fruit, reserving the port. Roast in a roasting pan at 350 degrees for 1$1/2$ hours or until cooked through, basting frequently with the reserved port. Boil any port left at the end of cooking and pour over the chicken before serving.

Yield: 10 servings
ANITA MAY

Betty and Robert Loeb

FLOSSIE BAYER'S CHICKEN FRICASSEE WITH MEATBALLS

1 chicken, cut up, skin removed
Salt and pepper to taste
1 (10³/4-ounce) can condensed
    cream of mushroom soup
1 (10³/4-ounce) can condensed
    cream of chicken soup
2 soup cans water

1 (1-ounce) envelope onion soup
    mix
3 to 4 ribs celery, chopped
1 pound ground beef
1 onion, finely chopped
1 to 2 ribs celery, finely chopped
Garlic powder to taste

Arrange the chicken in a baking dish. Season with salt and pepper. Mix the cream of mushroom soup, cream of chicken soup, water, onion soup mix and 3 to 4 ribs chopped celery in a bowl. Pour over the chicken. Cover and bake at 325 degrees for 45 minutes. Combine the ground beef, onion and finely chopped celery in a bowl. Season with salt, pepper and garlic powder. Mix with damp hands and form into small balls. Add to the chicken. Bake, uncovered, at 325 degrees for 30 minutes or until chicken and meatballs are cooked through. Serve over cooked white rice or matzo dressing.

Yield: 8 servings
GAIL BAYER (MRS. JEFFREY)

HONEY AND CURRY CHICKEN

¹/2 cup (1 stick) margarine, melted
¹/2 cup honey
¹/4 cup prepared yellow mustard
1 teaspoon curry powder

Dash of salt
4 to 6 boneless skinless chicken
    breasts

Mix the melted margarine, honey, prepared mustard, curry powder and salt in a shallow dish. Add chicken and turn to coat well. Arrange in a baking dish and cover. Bake at 425 degrees for 30 minutes. Uncover and bake for 15 minutes longer or until cooked through.

Yield: 4 to 6 servings
NANCY BERLAND

HONEY RITZ CHICKEN

Boneless skinless chicken breasts
Vegetable oil

Ritz crackers, crushed
Honey

Brush chicken breasts with oil and generously coat with cracker crumbs. Arrange in a baking dish. Bake at 350 degrees for 25 minutes. Drizzle honey generously over the chicken, covering well but don't soak with honey. Bake for 20 minutes longer or until cooked through and brown.

Yield: variable
MACKIE HOROWITZ

MOM'S EASY CHICKEN WITH PEGGY'S ORANGE CRANBERRY SAUCE

1 cup orange juice
1 cup sugar
12 ounces fresh cranberries
3/4 cup chopped pecans

1 chicken
Dijon mustard to taste
Seasoned salt to taste

Bring the orange juice and sugar to a boil in a saucepan. Add the cranberries. Cook, stirring often, until the cranberries pop. Remove from the heat and stir in the pecans. Chill, covered, for at least 3 hours.

Coat the chicken with Dijon mustard. Sprinkle with seasoned salt. Place on a rack in a roasting pan. Roast at 375 degrees for $1^{1}/_{2}$ to $2^{1}/_{2}$ hours or until cooked through. Serve with the cranberry sauce.

Yield: 4 to 6 servings
PEGGY BONFIELD

HERBED PAN-FRIED CHICKEN

2 to 3 tablespoons sea salt
1/4 cup sugar
1 1/2 teaspoons freshly ground pepper
1 tablespoon Cavender's all-purpose
    Greek seasoning
2 garlic bulbs, peeled
4 cups buttermilk
1 tablespoon hot red pepper sauce
3- to 4-pound roasting chicken, cut
    into 8 pieces

2 cups unbleached all-purpose flour
2 teaspoons freshly ground pepper
1/3 cup dried herb mixture (parsley,
    thyme, marjoram, chopped
    rosemary and basil)
1 egg
1 teaspoon baking powder
1/2 teaspoon baking soda
1 cup buttermilk
3 to 4 cups vegetable oil

Combine the sea salt, sugar, 1 1/2 teaspoons ground pepper and Cavender's in a large sealable plastic bag. Crush the garlic and add to the bag. Mix 4 cups buttermilk and hot red pepper sauce in a bowl and add to the bag. Add the chicken pieces and seal the bag. Marinate, chilled, for 2 to 3 hours or overnight, turning to coat. Remove chicken to a wire rack to drain; discard marinade. Combine the flour, 2 teaspoons ground pepper and herb mixture in a large plastic or brown paper bag. Beat the egg, baking powder, baking soda and 1 cup buttermilk in a shallow bowl. Dredge chicken in the flour mixture and shake off excess flour. Dip in the egg mixture; turn to coat. Drain excess egg and return to the flour mixture. Turn to coat. Remove excess flour and place on a wire rack.

Heat the oil in a heavy 12-inch cast-iron skillet to 375 degrees. Reduce the heat to medium and add the chicken, skin side down. Adjust the oil temperature to 300 degrees. Fry the chicken, covered, for 14 to 16 minutes. Turn the chicken. Fry the chicken, uncovered, for 14 to 16 minutes longer or until the skin is golden brown and the chicken is cooked through. Drain on a wire rack.

Temple Emanu-El of Birmingham, Alabama, is a Reform congregation, and there is a wide range of "Jewish Cooking" in our temple congregation. Some of our recipes do mix milk and meat. You can use a nondairy creamer in place of cream or milk in sauces even for meat dishes. There are a wide assortment of soy products that work very well to replace dairy products in meat dishes also. If butter appears in a meat recipe, a margarine that is labeled Parve, is an acceptable substitute, as well as a vegetable oil. Recipes that appear in this cookbook do not contain any *treyf* (forbidden foods under Jewish law).

Yield: 4 to 6 servings
SHERRON GOLDSTEIN

GREEK CHICKEN BREASTS

6 boneless chicken breast halves
3/4 cup olive oil
1/2 cup lemon juice
1/4 cup water
1 tablespoon garlic powder

1 teaspoon salt
1 teaspoon pepper
1 teaspoon chopped fresh basil
1 onion, sliced

Arrange the chicken breasts in a baking dish. Mix the olive oil, lemon juice and water in a bowl. Pour over the chicken. Sprinkle with the garlic powder, salt, pepper and basil. Top with the onion slices. Cover and bake at 375 degrees for 45 to 50 minutes or until cooked through.

Yield: 6 servings
GAIL HERMAN

MAMAW'S FRIED CHICKEN

1 chicken, cut up
2 eggs
2 cups crushed saltine crackers
Salt and pepper to taste
Garlic powder to taste

Rinse the chicken pieces and pat dry. Beat the eggs in a bowl. Place the cracker crumbs in a shallow dish. Season with salt, pepper and garlic powder. Dip the chicken in the beaten eggs and then roll in the cracker crumbs. Arrange on a baking sheet coated with vegetable oil. Bake at 325 degrees for 1 1/2 hours. Turn the chicken and bake for 30 minutes longer or until cooked through.

Yield: 4 to 6 servings
SUSAN KOPLON BARSTEIN

Sunday was the day! Every Sunday since my mom was old enough to remember, she would come home from Sunday school and smell the pleasant aromas of her mother's red kitchen. The favorite was my grandmother's famous oven-baked fried chicken. The secret ingredient was love and her old cookie sheets. My grandmother made this chicken along with her squash casserole, sweet-and-sour cabbage and twice-baked potatoes for family and friends! Her children, grandchildren, and great grandchildren enjoyed her famous chicken until my grandmother was in her nineties! She passed away this past November 2001 and in her mailbox (along with my mailbox) was this "generation to generation" letter—so I'm passing her recipe from Mamaw's kitchen to yours.

LEMON TARRAGON CHICKEN

2 tablespoons butter or margarine
8 boneless skinless chicken breasts
2 cups sliced fresh mushrooms
2 garlic cloves, minced
3 tablespoons dry sherry or white wine

1/2 teaspoon crushed dried tarragon
1/2 teaspoon lemon pepper
1 (14 1/2-ounce) can chicken broth
1/3 cup all-purpose flour
1/4 cup sour cream

Melt the butter in a 12-inch skillet over medium–high heat. Add the chicken, mushrooms, garlic, sherry, tarragon and lemon pepper. Cook for 10 to 12 minutes or until cooked through, turning once. Remove the chicken and mushrooms with a slotted spoon and keep warm. Combine the broth and flour in a jar with a tight-fitting lid. Shake until well mixed. Stir into the skillet and cook over medium–high heat until thickened and bubbly. Remove about 1/2 cup from the skillet and add to the sour cream in a bowl. Stir to blend and return to the skillet. Add the chicken and mushrooms and cook until heated through. Serve over hot cooked noodles.

Yield: 8 servings
BARBARA BERSCH NEWMAN

CHICKEN DIVAN

2 (10-ounce) packages frozen
    broccoli spears, cooked, drained
3 cups cooked rice
6 chicken breasts, cooked, cut into
    bite-size pieces
2 (10 3/4-ounce) cans condensed
    cream of chicken soup

1 cup mayonnaise
1/2 cup milk
1 teaspoon lemon juice
1/2 teaspoon curry powder
1 cup shredded New York cheese
1 cup herb-seasoned stuffing mix
2 tablespoons butter, melted

Arrange the broccoli spears in a buttered baking dish with the florets at the outside edges. Top with the rice and arrange the chicken pieces on the rice. Mix the next 5 ingredients in a bowl. Pour over the chicken. Sprinkle with the Cheddar cheese. Mix the stuffing mix and melted butter in a bowl. Sprinkle on top of the cheese. Bake at 350 degrees for 40 minutes.

Yield: 8 servings
PAT WEIL (MRS. LEONARD J.)

RUSSIAN CHICKEN

1/2 cup (1 stick) butter
8 chicken breasts
1 large onion, sliced
1 cup water
1/2 cup sherry

1/2 cup tomato juice
1 teaspoon salt
1 teaspoon paprika
Pepper to taste

Melt the butter in a large skillet. Add the chicken and cook until browned. Remove the chicken breasts with a slotted spoon to a roasting pan. Add the onion to the skillet. Sauté until translucent. Add to the chicken. Mix the water, sherry, tomato juice, salt and paprika in a bowl. Season with pepper. Pour over the chicken and onion. Bake at 400 degrees for 1¼ hours or until cooked through, turning every 30 minutes.

Yield: 8 servings
SHIRLEY LEADER

MIRIAM'S CHICKEN JUBILEE

4 (2½- to 3½-pound) chickens,
  cut up
2 teaspoons salt
1/4 teaspoon garlic salt
1 (12-ounce) bottle chili sauce
1/2 cup packed brown sugar
1/4 cup water

1 tablespoon Worcestershire sauce
8 ounces fresh mushrooms
2 onions, sliced
1 (16-ounce) can Bing cherries,
  drained
1/2 cup sherry

Arrange the chicken pieces on a broiler pan, skin side up. Sprinkle with the salt and garlic salt. Broil until browned. Remove to a large baking dish. Mix the chili sauce, brown sugar, water and Worcestershire sauce in a bowl. Pour over the chicken. Top with the mushrooms and onions. Bake at 325 degrees for about 45 minutes. Add the cherries and drizzle with the sherry. Bake for 15 minutes longer or until the chicken is cooked through. Serve over hot cooked rice.

The only thing I remember my mother cooking was French toast and it was always black. But mother gave this recipe to me and she told everyone that she taught me how to cook!

Yield: 12 servings
SALLIE DATNOFF DOWNS

CHICKEN NIÇOISE

2 (2¹/₂- to 3¹/₂-pound) chickens,
   cut up
Salt and pepper to taste
All-purpose flour
¹/₄ cup (¹/₂ stick) margarine (or more)
8 small onions
1 bell pepper, cut into strips
1 garlic clove, minced

4 tomatoes, peeled, seeded, chopped
1 bay leaf
¹/₄ teaspoon thyme
¹/₂ cup chicken broth
¹/₂ cup dry vermouth
8 ounces mushrooms
¹/₂ cup black olives
2 tablespoons chopped fresh parsley

Season the chicken pieces with salt and pepper. Add to a sealable plastic bag containing flour. Turn to coat. Remove the chicken, shaking off excess flour. Melt the margarine in a skillet. Add the chicken and sauté until browned. Remove to a baking dish using a slotted spoon or tongs. Add more margarine to the skillet if needed. Add the onions and sauté until browned. Remove to the baking dish. Add the bell pepper, garlic, tomatoes, bay leaf and thyme to the skillet. Sauté briefly being careful not to burn the garlic. Stir in the broth and vermouth. Cook, stirring up any browned bits, to deglaze the pan. Pour over the chicken and onions. Bake, covered, at 350 degrees for 30 minutes. Add the mushrooms. Bake for 30 minutes longer or until the chicken is cooked through; degrease before serving. Remove the bay leaf. Add the olives and sprinkle with the parsley before serving.

Yield: 8 servings
LENORE PICARD

Patsy and Charles Collat

CHICKEN WITH ALMONDS

1 (2 1/2- to 3 1/2-pound) chicken,
   cut up
1/4 cup (1/2 stick) butter
1 garlic clove, minced
2 tablespoons chopped onion
1 tablespoon tomato paste
2 tablespoons all-purpose flour

1 1/2 cups chicken stock or broth
2 tablespoons sherry
2 tablespoons slivered almonds
1 teaspoon tarragon
Salt and pepper to taste
3/4 cup sour cream
1 tablespoon grated Parmesan cheese

Brown the chicken pieces on all sides in the butter in a skillet. Remove to a plate. Add the garlic and onion to the skillet and sauté over low heat for 3 minutes. Add the tomato paste and flour and whisk until blended. Whisk in the stock and sherry. Return the chicken pieces when the mixture comes to a boil. Add the next 4 ingredients. Reduce the heat and cover. Simmer for 45 minutes or until the chicken is cooked through. Remove the chicken to a shallow heatproof baking dish. Stir the sour cream into the skillet. Cook until heated through but do not boil. Pour over the chicken and sprinkle with the Parmesan cheese. Place under a preheated broiler until lightly browned.

Yield: 4 servings
BARBARA A. ABRAMS

CHICKEN AND WILD RICE CASSEROLE

2 tablespoons margarine
1/2 cup chopped onion
1/2 cup chopped celery
1 (10 3/4-ounce) can condensed
   cream of mushroom soup
1/2 cup sour cream or nonfat plain
   yogurt

2/3 cup dry white wine
1/2 teaspoon curry powder
2 to 3 cups bite-size pieces cooked
   chicken
1 (6-ounce) package long grain and
   wild rice mix, cooked
1/4 cup chopped fresh parsley

Melt the margarine in a saucepan. Add the onion and celery and sauté until tender. Stir in the soup, sour cream, wine and curry powder. Add the chicken and rice and stir to mix. Spoon into a 7×12-inch baking dish. Bake at 350 degrees for 35 minutes. Sprinkle with the chopped parsley and serve.

Yield: 6 servings
NANCY GOEDECKE

THE SMOKED TURKEY

1/4 cup vegetable oil
1/2 cup salt
1/3 cup vinegar
1 tablespoon pepper

1/4 cup chopped fresh parsley
1 (12- to 16-pound) self-basting
turkey

Mix the oil, salt, vinegar, pepper and parsley in a bowl. Rub the outside and cavity of the turkey with this mixture. I use a standard dome smoker and a 10-pound bag of non-self-starting charcoal briquets. I stack the briquets forming a mound in the middle of the charcoal pan. I soak this mound with approximately 1/2 cup of lighter fluid and I light this. While the flame is burning, I do not cover the smoker. I then add six 2- to 3-inch chunks of hickory wood to the water pan, letting them soak. After the flame burns out and the coals are turning white (just in the middle of the charcoal pan), I place the wood chunks around the periphery of the charcoal. Then I place the water pan on the lower rack. I don't spread out the charcoal and occasionally I have added a can of beer to the water. It makes a little different taste. Then I place the rubbed turkey on the top portion of the grill and replace the heavy dome of the smoker. I don't uncover the turkey to check on it, but about 4 hours after initially placing the turkey on the rack, I do open the vent and add more water and charcoal. I time this so I put the turkey on about 7 p.m. I check it around 11 p.m. I leave it covered throughout the whole evening. At 7 a.m. the next morning, I am always surprised to see a golden brown smoked turkey. This is served with Helene's secret coleslaw with caraway seeds which will have to be included in the second edition of this cookbook. Serve with a spicy Zinfandel or a crisp Alsace Wine.

Yield: 16 to 20 servings
RICHARD ALAN ELKUS, M.D., P.A.

This is a family recipe that has been handed down from generation to generation for Smoked Turkey. I can trace the roots back to my Great, Great, Great Grandfather Chief Charging Elk. He prepared this for Miles Standish's son's Bar-Mitzvah.

RASHELLE AND JEREMY'S PACIFIC NORTHWEST SALMON

1/2 cup (1 stick) unsalted butter
1/3 cup honey
1/3 cup packed brown sugar
3 tablespoons fresh lemon juice

1 teaspoon crushed red pepper flakes
4 (6-ounce) salmon fillets
Vegetable oil

Combine the butter, honey, brown sugar, lemon juice and red pepper flakes in a saucepan. Cook over medium heat, stirring constantly, for 5 to 7 minutes or until smooth. Remove from the heat and let cool to room temperature. Arrange the salmon in a dish just large enough to hold it. Pour the cooled marinade over the salmon. Let stand for 30 minutes, turning once. Line the bottom of a broiling pan with foil. Brush the broiling rack with oil. Lay the fillets on the rack. Broil for 5 to 7 minutes, brushing once with the marinade. Turn the salmon and broil for 5 minutes or until the outside is slightly blackened and the inside is the desired doneness, brushing once with the marinade. Discard any remaining marinade.

Yield: 4 servings
LORAINE REZNIK

ORANGE BOURBON GRILLED SALMON

1/4 cup bourbon
1/4 cup fresh orange juice
1/4 cup low-sodium soy sauce
1/4 cup packed brown sugar
1/4 cup chopped green onions

3 tablespoons chopped fresh chives
2 tablespoons fresh lemon juice
2 garlic cloves, chopped
4 (6-ounce) salmon fillets, (about 1 inch thick)

Combine the bourbon, orange juice, soy sauce, brown sugar, green onions, chives, lemon juice and garlic in a large sealable plastic bag. Add the salmon and seal the bag. Marinate in the refrigerator for 1 1/2 hours, turning the bag occasionally. Remove the salmon to a broiler pan or grill rack coated with nonstick cooking spray. Reserve the marinade. Grill for 6 minutes per side or to the desired doneness, basting frequently with the reserved marinade. Discard any remaining marinade.

Yield: 4 servings
KAREN ALLEN

PAN-GRILLED SALMON WITH ROASTED PECANS

Olive oil	*Fresh lime juice*
Salmon fillet	*Roasted pecans*
Butter	

Pour just enough olive oil in the bottom of a grilling pan to cover the surface. Add the salmon and grill on both sides until the fish flakes easily. Remove to a serving platter. Top with a slice of butter and sprinkle with lime juice. Cover with roasted pecans.

Yield: 2 servings
SALLY GOLDSTEIN

BAKED FISH IN CHEESE CRACKERS

Cheese crackers	*Salt and pepper to taste*
Butter or margarine	*Lemon juice*
Crappie or bream fillets	*Lemon slices*

Crush the cheese crackers in a blender to a fine meal. Remove to a shallow dish. Line a baking pan with foil and grease with butter. Melt additional butter and pour into a shallow bowl. Season the fish with salt and pepper. Dip into the melted butter and then coat with cracker crumbs. Arrange on the foil in the baking pan. Sprinkle with lemon juice and top with lemon slices. Bake at 350 degrees until the fish flakes easily.

Yield: variable
SONYA D. LEFKOVITS

Norman Lefkovits (1909–1996) lived his entire life in Columbiana, AL. He died in the house in which he was born. Norman was an ardent fisherman. He liked to cook and eat the fish he caught. He loved cooking fish suppers for his friends in Columbiana and Birmingham. He fried his fish, baked them, and cooked them on the grill. His friend, Walton Lowry, who for years was the Birmingham News' Outdoor editor, printed this cheese fish recipe several times in his column in the Birmingham News.

NANA EDITH'S SALMON LOAF

2 (14³/4-ounce) cans red sockeye
   salmon, drained, flaked
2 eggs
1 onion, grated
Cornflake crumbs to taste

Sour cream to taste
Lemon juice to taste
Pepper to taste
Vegetable oil

Mix the salmon, eggs and onion in a bowl. Add cornflake crumbs to desired consistency. Season with sour cream, lemon juice and pepper. Pour a small amount of oil into a loaf pan. Heat at 350 degrees until hot, making sure the pan is coated with oil. Remove from the oven and carefully add the salmon mixture, forming a loaf. Bake at 350 degrees for 45 to 60 minutes.

Yield: 6 servings
NATALIE HAUSMAN-WEISS

ZUBIAC

16 ounces Monterey Jack cheese,
   shredded
1 cup grated Parmesan cheese
32 ounces small curd cottage cheese
2 eggs, beaten
1/2 cup (1 stick) butter, softened

1 tablespoon chopped fresh parsley
Salt and pepper to taste
Garlic salt to taste
8 ounces lasagna noodles, cooked
3 (10-ounce) packages frozen
   chopped spinach, cooked, drained

Mix the Monterey Jack cheese, Parmesan cheese, cottage cheese, eggs, melted butter and parsley in a large bowl. Season with salt, pepper and garlic salt. Arrange half the noodles in a greased 9x13-inch baking dish. Top with half the spinach and then half the cheese mixture. Repeat with the remaining noodles, spinach and cheese mixture. Bake at 350 degrees for 1 hour. Cut when cool. Can be frozen.

Yield: 12 servings
BARBARA BETTEN

LINGUINI WITH ARTICHOKES

1/4 cup olive oil
1/4 cup (1/2 stick) butter
1 tablespoon all-purpose flour
1 cup chicken broth, heated
1 garlic clove, crushed
2 teaspoons lemon juice
1 teaspoon finely chopped flat-leaf
    parsley

Salt and pepper to taste
2 (14 1/2-ounce) cans quartered
    artichoke hearts, drained
2 tablespoons (or more) grated
    Parmesan cheese
1 teaspoon (or more) drained capers
    (optional)
16 ounces linguini, cooked

Heat the olive oil in a skillet or large saucepan over medium heat. Add the
butter and heat until melted. Add the flour. Cook, stirring constantly, for a
few minutes. Stir in the heated broth and increase the heat to high. Cook for
1 minute. Stir in the garlic, lemon juice and parsley. Season with salt and pepper.
Reduce the heat to low and cook, stirring occasionally, for 5 minutes. Stir in the
artichoke hearts, Parmesan cheese and capers. Cook, covered, for about 8
minutes. Toss with hot linguini and serve.

Yield: 6 servings
CANDY MEYERSON

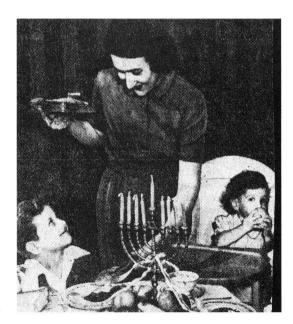

Candy Cotton Meyerson

SPAGHETTI BRAVISIMO

6 cups water
1 (1-ounce) envelope onion soup
   mix
8 ounces thin spaghetti
1 pound lean ground beef

1 (8-ounce) can tomato sauce
1 (6-ounce) can tomato paste
1 tablespoon dried parsley
1 teaspoon oregano
1/2 teaspoon basil

Heat the water to boiling in a large saucepan. Stir in the onion soup mix and spaghetti. Cook for 20 minutes or just until the pasta is tender. Remove from the heat but do not drain. Brown the ground beef in a skillet. Stir in the remaining ingredients. Add to the spaghetti and stir to mix. Cook until heated through. Serve with grated Parmesan cheese and a green salad.

Yield: 4 servings
Mrs. Herman Gotlieb

FUSILLI MICHELANGELO

2 to 4 tablespoons olive oil
8 ounces mushrooms (such as
   shiitake, porcini, cremini or
   chanterelles)
1 tablespoon minced garlic
2 (16-ounce) cans diced plum
   tomatoes, drained, juice reserved
1/2 cup thinly sliced drained
   oil-pack sun-dried tomatoes

1 tablespoon tomato paste
12 ounces fusilli, cooked al dente,
   drained
2 bunches arugula or basil, trimmed
1/2 cup (or more) grated Parmesan
   cheese
1/2 cup pine nuts, toasted
Salt and pepper to taste
Porcini oil (optional)

Heat the olive oil in a large skillet over medium-high heat. Add the mushrooms and sauté for 5 minutes or until golden brown. Add the garlic and sauté for 1 minute. Add the plum tomatoes, sun-dried tomatoes and tomato paste. Add a bit of reserved tomato juice if mixture seems too dry. Sauté for 3 minutes or until tomato juices begin to be released. Add the pasta, arugula, Parmesan cheese and pine nuts to the tomato mixture. Season with salt and pepper. Toss to mix. Cook until heated through. Sprinkle with porcini oil, if desired. Serve with a young cabernet.

Yield: 4 servings
Donna Goldberg

GEORGE'S FIG AND FETA SAUCE

1 tablespoon minced garlic	1/2 cup banana pepper brine
1 tablespoon olive oil	2 tablespoons butter
1 (14 1/2-ounce) can artichoke	2 tablespoons all-purpose flour
hearts, drained, chopped	1 cup milk
10 figs, chopped	2 teaspoons each oregano and thyme
10 pitted black olives, chopped	8 ounces feta cheese, crumbled
10 jarred banana peppers, chopped	3 green onions, sliced

Sauté the garlic briefly in the olive oil in a large skillet. Add the next 5 ingredients. Cook, stirring occasionally, until all the liquid evaporates. Push the mixture to one side of the skillet. Melt the butter on the empty side. Add the flour. Cook until the butter is absorbed and the mixture begins to brown, stirring constantly. Stir the milk slowly into the flour mixture. Cook until thickened. Stir in the oregano and thyme. Move the artichoke mixture into the sauce and stir to mix. Remove from the heat and add the feta cheese and green onions. Stir until the cheese melts. Serve warm over pasta or rice.

Yield: 4 main dish servings
GEORGE THOMPSON

TURKEY SPAGHETTI SAUCE

Chopped onions and minced garlic	Worcestershire sauce for chicken,
Olive oil	salt-free lemon pepper, Italian
Ground turkey	seasoning, cooking wine or
1 (14 1/2-ounce) can no-salt-added	sherry, chopped fresh parsley and
whole tomatoes	sliced fresh mushrooms to taste
1 (6-ounce) can no-salt-added	Cooked spaghetti
tomato paste	

Sauté the onions and garlic in the olive oil in a large skillet until translucent. Add the ground turkey and sauté until cooked through. Add the tomatoes; break apart with a spoon. Stir in the tomato paste. Stir in the remaining ingredients except spaghetti. Simmer until the mushrooms are cooked. Serve over hot spaghetti.

Yield: 4 servings
KAYDEE ERDREICH BREMEN

Vegetarian Spaghetti Sauce

Extra-virgin olive oil
6 onions
1 garlic bulb, separated into cloves,
    peeled
1 pound baby carrots
1 bunch celery
3 red bell peppers
3 yellow bell peppers
8 summer squash
6 zucchini
18 plum tomatoes
24 ounces fresh mushrooms
Kosher salt and black pepper to taste

Lemon pepper to taste
Oregano to taste
Basil to taste
Sugar to taste
3 bay leaves
1 (16-ounce) can tomato juice
3 to 4 (26-ounce) jars Ragu
    traditional spaghetti sauce
1 (26-ounce) jar Newman's Own
    Hot & Spicy spaghetti sauce
2 (6-ounce) cans (or more) tomato
    paste

Add olive oil to a very large stockpot coated with nonstick cooking spray. Chop the onions, garlic, carrots, celery, red bell peppers, yellow bell peppers, squash, zucchini, tomatoes and mushrooms in batches in a food processor until finely chopped. Add to the stockpot. Season with kosher salt, black pepper, lemon pepper, oregano, basil and sugar. Add the bay leaves. Bring to a simmer and cook for 30 to 45 minutes, stirring often. Skim off the liquid. Stir in the tomato juice, Ragu spaghetti sauce, Newman's Own spaghetti sauce and tomato paste. Cook for at least 1 hour, stirring often.

Yield: 10 to 12 quarts
KAREN ALLEN

Brunch & Bread

BREAKFAST EGG CASSEROLE

16 ounces cottage cheese
16 ounces sharp Cheddar cheese,
  shredded
1/2 cup (1 stick) butter, melted
1/2 large onion, grated
8 ounces mushrooms, sliced
1 tablespoon Dijon mustard
Dash of red pepper flakes

12 eggs
1/2 cup all-purpose flour
1 teaspoon baking powder
1 teaspoon salt
1/2 teaspoon pepper
2 tomatoes, sliced
Finely chopped fresh parsley

Combine the cottage cheese, Cheddar cheese, melted butter, onion, mushrooms, Dijon mustard and red pepper flakes in a large bowl. Beat the eggs, flour, baking powder, salt and pepper in a bowl until frothy. Add to the cheese mixture and mix well. Pour into a 9×13-inch baking dish coated with nonstick cooking spray. Arrange the tomato slices on top and sprinkle with chopped parsley. Bake at 325 to 350 degrees for 45 to 60 minutes.

Yield: 10 to 12 servings
BABS PERLMAN

MINI SPINACH QUICHES

2 cups all-purpose flour
1 cup (2 sticks) butter, softened
6 ounces cream cheese, softened
3 eggs, beaten

1 cup chopped spinach
1 cup shredded Swiss cheese
1 cup light cream

Mix the flour, butter and cream cheese in a bowl until well blended. Form into 48 small balls and press into the bottom and sides of mini muffin tins. Mix the eggs, spinach, Swiss cheese and cream in a bowl. Spoon into the prepared crusts to the top. Bake at 400 degrees for 15 to 18 minutes.

Yield: 4 dozen mini quiches
DEBBY THOMAS

MEXICAN QUICHE

2 tablespoons margarine, melted
10 eggs, well beaten
1/2 cup all-purpose flour
1 teaspoon baking powder
1 teaspoon salt
2 (4-ounce) cans chopped
  green chiles

16 ounces cottage cheese
16 ounces Monterey Jack cheese,
  shredded
3 or 4 tomatoes, chopped

Mix the margarine, eggs, flour, baking powder, salt, green chiles, cottage cheese, Monterey Jack cheese and chopped tomatoes in a bowl. Pour into a 9×13-inch baking dish. Bake at 400 degrees for 15 minutes. Reduce the oven temperature to 350 degrees and bake for 25 minutes longer. Let stand for 15 minutes before serving.

Note: You may substitute up to half the eggs with an equivalent amount of egg substitute.

Yield: 10 to 12 servings
FRANCES G. CYPRESS

MAWMAW'S BISCUITS

2 1/2 cups all-purpose flour
1 teaspoon salt
2 1/2 teaspoons baking powder

1 cup shortening
1 cup plus 2 tablespoons buttermilk
Melted butter

Sift the flour, salt and baking powder into a large bowl. Cut in the shortening with a pastry blender or fork. Add the buttermilk and stir until blended. Roll out the dough on a lightly floured surface. Brush with melted butter and fold in half. Cut with a biscuit cutter. Place biscuits on a baking sheet and brush tops with melted butter. Bake at 450 degrees for 15 minutes.

Yield: (about) 3 dozen biscuits
CHU-CHI FIERMAN

BLUEBERRY MUFFINS

2 cups all-purpose flour
1/2 cup sugar
1 tablespoon baking powder
1 teaspoon cinnamon
1/2 teaspoon salt

1 egg
1 cup milk
3 tablespoons butter, softened
1 tablespoon vanilla extract
1 cup blueberries

Mix the flour, sugar, baking powder, cinnamon and salt in a bowl. Beat the egg, milk and butter in a mixing bowl. Beat in the vanilla. Make a well in the center of the flour mixture. Pour the egg mixture into the well. Stir until well moistened, but not smooth. Fold in the blueberries. Spoon the batter into greased muffin tins, filling them two-thirds full. Bake at 400 degrees for 20 to 30 minutes or until golden brown. Remove to a wire rack to cool.

Yield: 12 muffins
SARAH HALPERN

REFRIGERATOR BRAN MUFFINS

2 cups Raisin Bran cereal
1 1/4 cups all-purpose flour
3/4 cup sugar
1 1/4 teaspoons baking soda
1/2 teaspoon salt
1/4 teaspoon ground cloves

1/4 teaspoon cinnamon
1/4 teaspoon nutmeg
1 egg
1 cup buttermilk
1/4 cup vegetable oil
1/2 teaspoon vanilla extract

Mix the cereal, flour, sugar, baking soda, salt, cloves, cinnamon and nutmeg in a bowl. Beat the egg, buttermilk, oil and vanilla in a bowl. Add to the dry ingredients and stir to mix. Spoon into muffin tins. Bake at 400 degrees for 15 minutes.

Note: The batter can be kept in the refrigerator for up to 3 weeks.

Yield: (about) 14 muffins
JEANNE HAGEDORN

CHOCOLATE CHIP COFFEE CAKE

1 cup semisweet chocolate chips	1 teaspoon vanilla extract
1/4 cup water	2 cups flour
2/3 cup shortening	1 tablespoon instant coffee crystals
1 1/4 cups sugar	1 teaspoon baking powder
3 eggs	1/4 teaspoon baking soda
2/3 cup water	Pinch of salt

Combine the chocolate chips and 1/4 cup water in a saucepan. Cook over low heat until the chocolate melts. Set aside. Beat the shortening, sugar and eggs in a bowl. Beat in 2/3 cup water and vanilla until creamy. Sift the flour, coffee crystals, baking powder, baking soda and salt in a bowl. Add the dry ingredients gradually to the shortening mixture and beat until blended. Pour half the batter into a greased 10-inch tube pan. Top with 3/4 of the melted chocolate mixture. Add the remaining batter and top with the remaining chocolate mixture. Run a knife carefully through the batter to swirl. Bake at 350 degrees for 35 to 45 minutes or until a wooden pick inserted in the center comes out clean. Remove to a wire rack to cool.

Yield: 10 to 12 servings

MACKIE HOROWITZ

PAULINE'S DANISH COFFEE CAKE

1 cup (2 sticks) butter, melted
2 tablespoons sugar
3 egg yolks
2 envelopes dry yeast
1/2 cup lukewarm milk
2 1/2 cups all-purpose flour
3 egg whites

1 cup sugar
Cinnamon to taste
Sugar to taste
Raisins to taste
Chopped nuts to taste
Melted butter to taste

Mix 1 cup melted butter, 2 tablespoons sugar and egg yolks in a bowl. Dissolve the yeast in the milk in a bowl. Add to the melted butter mixture and stir to blend. Stir in the flour to form a soft dough. Chill, covered, overnight. Divide the dough into 3 or 4 balls. Roll out each on a lightly floured surface. Beat the egg whites in a mixing bowl until stiff. Beat in 1 cup sugar. Spread the egg white mixture on the rolled out dough. Sprinkle each with cinnamon, sugar to taste, raisins and nuts. Roll up and place on a greased baking sheet. Brush with melted butter to taste and sprinkle with cinnamon and sugar to taste. Cover and let stand at room temperature for 2 hours. Bake at 350 degrees for 30 minutes. Slice when cool.

Yield: 12 servings
GLADYS EPSTEIN

Alex and Gladys Epstein

QUICK SOUR CREAM COFFEE CAKE

1 (18¼-ounce) package yellow
  cake mix
4 eggs
1 cup vegetable oil
1 cup sour cream
1 (6-ounce) package vanilla instant
  pudding mix
1 teaspoon vanilla extract
Dash of salt

6 tablespoons all-purpose flour
½ cup sugar
½ cup packed brown sugar
1 cup chopped pecans
1 teaspoon cinnamon, or
  ½ teaspoon cinnamon and
  ½ teaspoon nutmeg or ginger
½ cup (1 stick) butter or margarine

Beat the cake mix, eggs, oil, sour cream, pudding mix, vanilla and salt in a bowl with an electric mixer for 7 minutes. Pour half the batter into a greased and floured 9×13-inch cake pan. Mix the flour, sugar, brown sugar, pecans and cinnamon in a bowl. Cut in the butter until crumbly. Sprinkle half the streusel topping over the batter in the pan. Add the rest of the batter and sprinkle with the remaining streusel. Bake at 350 degrees for 45 to 60 minutes or until a wooden pick inserted in the center comes out clean. Check after 50 minutes; do not overbake. Remove to a wire rack. Cut into squares when cool. Chill for easier cutting.

Yield: 12 servings
CAROL F. HERMAN

This delicious, easy coffee cake recipe was given to me 35 years ago by Arene Nussbaum, the beautiful, dear wife of Jackson, Mississippi's Rabbi Perry Nussbaum. Now the third generation of Hermans is making and enjoying this great recipe. It is always a favorite at family gatherings.

Sunny's Coffee Cake

1/2 cup (1 stick) butter, softened
1 cup sugar
2 eggs
2 cups all-purpose flour
2 teaspoons baking powder

3/4 cup evaporated milk
1 teaspoon vanilla extract
Sugar to taste
Cinnamon to taste
Pecan pieces to taste

Beat the butter and 1 cup sugar in a bowl. Beat in the eggs 1 at a time. Add the flour and baking powder and mix well. Stir in the evaporated milk and vanilla. Pour the batter into a 9-inch cake pan. Sprinkle with sugar to taste, cinnamon and pecan pieces. Bake at 350 degrees for 35 to 40 minutes or until a wooden pick inserted in the center comes out clean. Remove to a wire rack to cool.

Yield: 8 servings
Cathy O. Friedman

My mother, Sunny Ovson, made her signature coffee cake for many occasions—card games, parties, etc. I remember that she would always go to the kitchen to bake immediately after hearing of the loss of a friend or family member. She would always arrive at the house of mourning with a warm coffee cake. Mother took over her cake to the home of a dear friend whose son had been tragically killed in a car accident. Her friend had been unable to eat a bite of food, but was able to eat a piece of mother's cake filled with so much love and care.

SCHNECKEN

1 cake yeast or 1 envelope dry yeast	Grated zest of $1/2$ lemon
2 cups lukewarm milk	7 cups all-purpose flour
1 cup all-purpose flour	Melted butter
1 cup (2 sticks) butter, softened	Sugar to taste
1 cup sugar	Cinnamon to taste
4 eggs	$1/2$ cup raisins
1 teaspoon salt	

Crumble the yeast into a bowl. Stir in the milk and 1 cup flour. Set in a warm place to rise. Beat softened butter and 1 cup sugar in a bowl. Add the eggs 1 at a time, mixing well after each addition. Stir in the salt and lemon zest. Add the yeast mixture alternately with 7 cups flour and mix well. Turn out onto a lightly floured surface. Knead until smooth and elastic. Let rise in a warm place until doubled in size. Roll out the dough to an oblong sheet about 9 inches wide and $1/4$ inch thick on a lightly floured surface. Brush generously with melted butter. Sprinkle with sugar to taste, cinnamon and raisins. Roll up as for a jelly roll and slice. Brush sides with melted butter. Arrange the slices flat side down close together in a shallow buttered baking pan. Brush the tops with melted butter. Sprinkle with cinnamon and sugar to taste. Let rise until doubled in bulk. Bake at 350 degrees for 20 to 25 minutes.

Yield: 8 servings

ROSALIE BLACH GOTLIEB

My most cherished cookbook is the Settlement Cookbook, *copyright 1943, which belonged to my mother, Rosalie Blach. Mother made many wonderful recipes from this cookbook, but one in particular, Schnecken, a warm sticky cinnamon roll, stands out in my memory as a favorite. She would make these for us on cold winter mornings and sometimes they would be cooling as we got home from school for an afternoon snack. Schnecken is prepared in two parts, the first being a Kuchen Dough, and the second being the bun or roll itself. Because of her notations in the margin, I know which recipes she used and if they were modified. Also the most soiled pages are obviously her favorites and are now mine and those of my family.*

GRANDMA SARAH'S BANANA BREAD

1 cup (2 sticks) margarine, softened
2 1/4 cups sugar
3 eggs
1 cup sour cream
3 ripe bananas, mashed
1 teaspoon vanilla extract

3 cups all-purpose flour
1 teaspoon baking powder
1 teaspoon baking soda
Pinch of salt
3/4 cup ground nuts

Beat the margarine and sugar in a bowl. Add the eggs and mix well. Stir in the sour cream, bananas and vanilla. Combine the flour, baking powder, baking soda and salt in a bowl. Stir into the banana mixture. Add the nuts and stir until well mixed. Pour the batter into 2 greased and floured loaf pans. Bake at 350 degrees for 1 hour or until a wooden pick inserted in the center comes out clean. Remove to a wire rack to cool.

Yield: 2 loaves
SUSAN BARSTEIN

BANANA CHOCOLATE CHIP LOAF

3 ripe bananas
1/2 cup (1 stick) butter or margarine, melted
1 cup sugar
2 eggs
1 teaspoon vanilla extract

2 cups all-purpose flour
1 teaspoon baking soda
1/4 teaspoon salt
3/4 cup semisweet chocolate chips
Confectioners' sugar to taste

Combine the bananas, melted butter, sugar, eggs and vanilla in a food processor or blender. Process until blended. Add the flour, baking soda and salt. Process until well mixed. Fold in the chocolate chips. Pour the batter into a greased 5×9-inch loaf pan. Bake at 350 degrees for 1 hour or until a wooden pick inserted in the center comes out clean. Let cool. Remove from the pan and dust with confectioners' sugar. Wrap tightly in foil. Freezes well.

Yield: 1 loaf
AMY SAAG
IRMA KOCH

PUMPKIN BREAD

2 cups sugar
1 cup vegetable oil
2 eggs
2 cups canned pumpkin
3 cups all-purpose flour

1 teaspoon baking powder
1 teaspoon baking soda
1 teaspoon cinnamon
1/2 cup milk
1 teaspoon vanilla extract

Mix the sugar, oil, eggs and pumpkin in a bowl. Sift the flour, baking powder, baking soda and cinnamon into a bowl. Mix the milk and vanilla in a small bowl. Add the dry ingredients to the pumpkin mixture alternately with the milk mixture, mixing well after each addition. Pour the batter into 2 greased loaf pans. Bake at 350 degrees for 1 hour or until a wooden pick inserted in the center comes out clean. Remove to a wire rack to cool.

Yield: 2 loaves
CEIL SUNDOCK

SOUTHERN CORN BREAD

5 handfuls cornmeal
1 egg
1 teaspoon baking powder

1 cup (about) buttermilk
Vegetable oil

Mix the cornmeal, egg, baking powder and enough buttermilk in a bowl to make a batter. Coat the bottom of a cast-iron skillet with oil. Heat at 350 degrees until the oil is hot. Pour the batter into the hot skillet. Bake at 350 degrees for 20 to 30 minutes or until golden brown and a wooden pick inserted in the center comes out clean. Serve warm with butter.

Yield: 8 servings
JULIE WATSON

Desserts

APRICOT POUND CAKE

3 cups all-purpose flour
1/2 teaspoon baking soda
Pinch of salt
1 cup sour cream
1 teaspoon vanilla extract
1 teaspoon orange extract

3/4 teaspoon rum flavoring
1/2 cup apricot brandy
1 cup (2 sticks) margarine, softened
3 cups sugar
6 eggs

Sift the flour, baking soda and salt into a bowl. Mix the sour cream, vanilla, orange extract, rum flavoring and apricot brandy in a bowl. Beat the margarine and sugar in a large bowl until light and fluffy. Add the eggs 1 at a time, beating well after each addition. Add the dry ingredients alternately with the sour cream mixture, mixing well after each addition. Pour into a greased and floured long loaf pan. Bake at 325 degrees for 1 hour and 20 minutes to 1 hour and 30 minutes or until a wooden pick inserted in the center comes out clean. Remove to a wire rack to cool.

Yield: 1 loaf
JANE BLUESTEIN

MIMI'S POUND CAKE

2 cups (4 sticks) butter (or half
  margarine), softened
3 cups sugar
6 eggs, at room temperature

3/4 cup milk, at room temperature
2 teaspoons vanilla extract
4 cups cake flour, sifted

Beat the butter and sugar in a large bowl until light and fluffy. Add the eggs 1 at a time, beating well after each addition. Combine the milk and vanilla in a small bowl. Add the cake flour to the butter mixture alternately with the milk mixture, beginning and ending with the cake flour. Pour into a greased and floured 10-inch tube pan. Bake at 300 degrees for 1 hour and 40 minutes or until a wooden pick inserted in the center comes out clean. Cool in the pan for 10 minutes. Invert onto a wire rack to cool completely.

Yield: 10 servings
GAIL HERMAN

CHOCOLATE ICEBOX CAKE

12 ounces German's sweet chocolate
6 to 9 tablespoons water
3 cups whipping cream

1 to 2 teaspoons vanilla extract
1 to 2 teaspoons sugar
24 ladyfingers

Combine the chocolate and water in a saucepan. Cook over low heat until the chocolate melts, stirring occasionally. Remove from the heat and let cool until thickened. Whip the cream, vanilla and sugar in a bowl. Fold in the cooled chocolate mixture. Line the bottom and side of a 9-inch springform pan with the ladyfingers. Pour the chocolate mixture into the pan. Chill for several hours.

Yield: 8 to 10 servings
ANNE SILBERMAN
JEAN SKLAR

CHOCOLATE SHEET CAKE

2 cups all-purpose flour
2 cups sugar
1 cup (2 sticks) butter
1/4 cup baking cocoa
1 cup cold water

1/2 cup sour cream
2 eggs, beaten
1 teaspoon baking soda
1 teaspoon vanilla extract

Sift the flour and sugar into a large bowl. Combine the butter, baking cocoa and water in a saucepan. Bring to a boil, stirring occasionally. Pour over the flour mixture and stir well. Stir in the sour cream, eggs, baking soda and vanilla. Pour into a 10×15-inch cake pan. Bake at 400 degrees for 20 minutes or until a wooden pick inserted in the center comes out clean. Remove to a wire rack and poke holes in the surface with a fork. Spread Chocolate Icing, Chocolate Pecan Frosting or Brownie Cake Icing over the hot sheet cake. Let cool in the pan.

Yield: 15 servings
LYNNE COHEN

CHOCOLATE ICING

1/2 cup (1 stick) margarine
1/4 cup baking cocoa
6 tablespoons milk

1 teaspoon vanilla extract
1 (16-ounce) box confectioners' sugar

Combine the margarine, baking cocoa, milk and vanilla in a saucepan. Bring to a simmer. Stir in the confectioners' sugar. Spread over the hot sheet cake.

LYNNE COHEN

CHOCOLATE PECAN FROSTING

3/4 cup (1 1/2 sticks) margarine
2 heaping tablespoons baking cocoa
1 (16-ounce) box confectioners'
    sugar, sifted

1/2 cup chopped pecans
6 tablespoons milk
1 tablespoon vanilla extract

Melt the margarine and baking cocoa in a saucepan over low heat. Heat to almost simmering, stirring constantly. Beat in the confectioners' sugar. Add the pecans, milk and vanilla and beat well. Spread over the hot sheet cake.

RONNE AND DONALD HESS

BROWNIE CAKE ICING

1/2 cup (1 stick) butter
1/3 cup evaporated milk
1/4 cup baking cocoa

1 (16-ounce) box confectioners' sugar
1 teaspoon vanilla extract
1 cup pecan pieces (optional)

Combine the butter, evaporated milk and baking cocoa in a saucepan. Bring to a boil. Remove from the heat and stir in the confectioners' sugar. Reduce the heat to low and cook, stirring constantly, until the icing is smooth. Remove from the heat and stir in the vanilla and pecan pieces. Spread over the hot sheet cake.

JANE SEIGEL

CHOCOLATE RIBBON CAKE

Cream Cheese Filling
8 ounces cream cheese, softened
2 tablespoons butter, softened
1/4 cup sugar
1 tablespoon cornstarch
1 egg
1/4 cup milk
1 teaspoon vanilla extract

Icing
1 cup sugar
3 tablespoons cornstarch
2 ounces bittersweet chocolate
Pinch of salt
1 cup boiling water
3 tablespoons butter
1 teaspoon vanilla extract

Batter
2 cups all-purpose flour
1 teaspoon baking powder
1/2 teaspoon baking soda
1/2 teaspoon salt
1/2 cup (1 stick) butter, softened
2 cups sugar
2 eggs
1 1/3 cups milk
1 teaspoon vanilla extract
4 (1-ounce) packets Choco Bake

For the filling, beat the cream cheese, butter, sugar, cornstarch, egg, milk and vanilla in a bowl until creamy. Set aside.

For the batter, sift the flour, baking powder, baking soda and salt into a bowl. Beat the butter and sugar in a large bowl until light and fluffy. Add the eggs 1 at a time, beating well after each addition. Add the dry ingredients alternately with the milk and beat well. Add the vanilla and Choco Bake and mix well. Pour half the batter into a greased and floured tube pan. Top with the cream cheese filling. Pour the remaining batter over the filling. Bake at 350 degrees for 1 hour and 10 minutes or until a wooden pick inserted in the center comes out clean. Remove to a wire rack to cool. Invert onto a serving plate.

For the icing, combine the sugar, cornstarch, chocolate and salt in a saucepan. Stir in the boiling water gradually. Cook over medium heat, stirring constantly until thick. Remove from the heat and stir in the butter and vanilla. Spread over the cooled cake.

Yield: 10 servings
LETTY MARCUS

MOLTEN CHOCOLATE CAKE

Sauce

4 1/2 ounces bittersweet or semisweet
    chocolate, chopped
2 ounces unsweetened chocolate,
    chopped
1/3 cup hot water
1/4 cup light corn syrup
1/4 teaspoon peppermint extract

Cake

5 ounces bittersweet or semisweet
    chocolate, chopped
10 tablespoons (1 1/4 sticks) butter
3 eggs
3 egg yolks
1 1/2 cups confectioners' sugar
1/2 cup all-purpose flour

For the sauce, melt the bittersweet and unsweetened chocolate in the top of a double boiler over gently simmering water. Add the hot water, corn syrup and peppermint extract and whisk until smooth. Remove from the heat and let cool slightly. May be made up to 2 days ahead. Chill, covered, until ready to serve. Reheat gently before serving.

For the cake, combine the bittersweet chocolate and butter in a heavy saucepan. Cook over medium heat, stirring constantly, until melted. Remove from the heat and let cool slightly. Whisk the eggs and egg yolks in a large bowl. Whisk in the confectioners' sugar. Whisk in the chocolate mixture and flour. Pour the batter into six 6-ounce custard cups coated with nonstick cooking spray or butter. May be made 1 day ahead. Chill, covered, until ready to bake. Arrange the custard cups on a baking sheet. Bake at 450 degrees for 11 minutes (or up to 14 minutes for refrigerated batter) or until the sides are set but the centers are soft. Run a small knife around the edge of the cups to loosen the cakes. Invert onto dessert plates and spoon the sauce around the cakes. Serve with mint chocolate chip ice cream.

Yield: 6 servings
LORAINE REZNIK

*Letty and Bob Marcus Family
(left to right):
Audrey and Denny Schnabl,
Bob and Letty, Suzy and Bill
Goldberg, Nathan and Julie Marcus,
Sandye Lichtenstein Lewis,
Julian Goldberg, Alexis Marcus,
Elliot Schnabl, Rachael Marcus,
Jacquelyn Goldberg, Matthew Marcus*

CHOCOLATE MARBLE

1 1/2 cups (3 sticks) butter, softened
2 cups sugar
4 eggs
1 cup milk
3 cups all-purpose flour

4 teaspoons baking powder
4 ounces chocolate, grated
1 teaspoon cinnamon
1 teaspoon vanilla extract

Beat the butter and sugar in a bowl until light and fluffy. Add the eggs 1 at a time, beating well after each addition. Beat in the milk. Add the flour and baking powder and beat until smooth. Remove 1/3 of the batter to another bowl. Add the chocolate, cinnamon and vanilla to the smaller amount of batter and stir to mix well. Pour a layer of white batter in a greased tube pan. Add the chocolate batter by spoonfuls. Top with the remaining white batter. Bake at 350 degrees for 45 minutes or until a wooden pick inserted in the center comes out clean. Remove to a wire rack to cool.

Yield: 8 to 10 servings
JOAN AND JACK BECKER

Joan and Jack Becker

Cake

4 cups all-purpose flour
2 tablespoons baking powder
1 cup (2 sticks) butter, softened
2 cups sugar
4 eggs
1¹/2 cups milk
2 teaspoons vanilla extract

Caramel Icing

3 cups sugar
¹/4 cup (¹/2 stick) butter
1¹/4 cups whole milk or light cream
1 cup sugar

For the cake, sift the flour and baking powder into a bowl 3 times. Beat the butter and sugar in a bowl until light and fluffy. Add the eggs 1 at a time, beating well after each addition. Add the dry ingredients alternately with the milk and beat well. Stir in the vanilla. Pour into three 9-inch round cake pans. Bake at 375 degrees for 25 to 30 minutes or until a wooden pick inserted in the center comes out clean. Remove to a wire rack to cool.

For the icing, combine 3 cups sugar, butter and milk in a saucepan. Heat slowly until hot. Heat 1 cup sugar in a skillet until it melts and becomes golden brown, stirring constantly. Add the caramelized sugar slowly to the saucepan when the first mixture begins to boil. Cook until the mixture reaches 234 degrees on a candy thermometer, about 25 to 30 minutes. Remove from the heat and beat until glossy. Spread on the cake when cool.

Yield: 8 servings
RHODA KAPLAN

Bessie Siegal's grandchildren enjoy a meal in her home. Left to right: Sandy, Judy, Debbie, Susan, Kenny, and Frank Siegal are ready to be served.

1-2-3-4 CAKE

1 cup (2 sticks) butter, softened
2 cups sugar
4 egg yolks, well beaten
1 teaspoon vanilla extract

3 cups all-purpose flour
4 teaspoons baking powder
1 cup milk
4 egg whites

Beat the butter and sugar in a large bowl until light and fluffy. Beat in the egg yolks and vanilla. Sift the flour and baking powder into a bowl. Add the dry ingredients to the butter mixture alternately with the milk, beating well after each addition. Beat the egg whites in a bowl until stiff. Fold into the batter. Pour the batter into muffin tins, 2 cake pans or a loaf pan. Bake at 375 degrees for 15 to 20 minutes for muffins, 365 degrees for 15 to 25 minutes for layers or 325 to 350 degrees for 40 to 45 minutes for a loaf or until a wooden pick inserted in the center comes out clean.

Yield: 8 servings
DODIE JAFFE AND JUDY BORISKY

The Held Family

114

RED VELVET CAKE WITH CREAM CHEESE FROSTING

Cake

1/2 cup shortening
1 1/2 cups sugar
2 eggs
2 ounces red food coloring
2 tablespoons baking cocoa
2 1/4 cups all-purpose flour
1 scant teaspoon salt
1 cup buttermilk
1 teaspoon vanilla extract
1 teaspoon butter flavoring
1 teaspoon baking soda
1 tablespoon vinegar

Frosting

8 ounces cream cheese, softened
1/4 cup (1/2 stick) margarine,
    softened
1 teaspoon vanilla extract
1 (16-ounce) box confectioners' sugar

For the cake, beat the shortening, sugar and eggs in a large bowl until light and fluffy. Stir the food coloring and baking cocoa in a small bowl to make a paste. Add to the shortening mixture and stir to blend. Beat in the flour, salt, buttermilk, vanilla and butter flavoring. Add the baking soda and vinegar and stir just to blend. Pour the batter into 3 greased and floured round cake pans. Bake at 350 degrees for 30 minutes or until a wooden pick inserted in the center comes out clean. Remove to a wire rack to cool.

For the frosting, beat the cream cheese, margarine and vanilla in a bowl until light and fluffy. Beat in the confectioners' sugar gradually and beat until smooth. Spread on the cooled cake.

Yield: 12 servings
RONNE AND DONALD HESS

Nanny's Pineapple Upside-Down Cake

1¾ cups all-purpose flour
2 teaspoons baking powder
¼ teaspoon salt
⅓ cup butter, softened
1 cup sugar
2 eggs, well beaten

½ cup milk or pineapple juice
1 teaspoon vanilla extract
2 tablespoons butter
1 cup packed brown sugar
Canned sliced or crushed pineapple,
    drained

Sift the flour, baking powder and salt into a bowl. Beat ⅓ cup butter and the sugar in a large bowl until light and fluffy. Add the eggs and beat well. Add the dry ingredients alternately with the milk and beat well. Stir in the vanilla. Melt 2 tablespoons butter in a cast-iron skillet. Add the brown sugar. Cook, stirring constantly, until smooth. Remove from the heat. Arrange a layer of sliced or crushed pineapple on the brown sugar. Top with the batter. Bake at 375 degrees for 45 minutes or until a wooden pick inserted in the center comes out clean. Remove to a wire rack to cool for a few minutes. Invert onto a serving platter and let cool. Serve with spiced whipped cream.

Yield: 8 servings
NANCY DENNEY

Rosalyn and Irvin Siegal and their seven grandchildren.
Top Row (left to right): Alex Lipow, Nicole Siegal, Andrew Siegal, Sammy Siegal.
Bottom Row (left to right): Irvin Siegal, Alison Siegal, Rosalyn Siegal, Tori Siegal

PISTACHIO CAKE

1 (18¹/4-ounce) package yellow cake
   mix
1 (4-ounce) package pistachio
   pudding mix
¹/2 cup vegetable oil

4 eggs
1 cup sour cream
¹/2 cup chopped pecans
³/4 cup Hershey's chocolate syrup

Beat the cake mix, pudding mix, oil, eggs and sour cream in a bowl until well mixed. Sprinkle the pecans in the bottom of a greased and floured bundt pan. Add half the batter to the pan. Stir the chocolate syrup into the remaining batter and add to the bundt pan. Swirl the batter gently with a fork. Bake at 375 degrees for 40 minutes or until a wooden pick inserted in the center comes out clean. Remove to a wire rack to cool.

Yield: 16 servings
MARION LEAF
MRS. ISADORE EUBANKS

NUT AND DATE CAKE

1 cup all-purpose flour
1 cup sugar
2 teaspoons baking powder
¹/2 teaspoon salt
1 pound walnuts, chopped

1 pound pitted dates, halved
5 egg yolks
1 teaspoon vanilla extract
5 egg whites

Mix the flour, sugar, baking powder and salt in a large bowl. Stir in the walnuts and dates. Beat the egg yolks and vanilla in a bowl until pale yellow. Add to the dry ingredients and mix well. Beat the egg whites in a bowl until soft peaks form. Fold gently into the batter. Pour into a well-greased tube pan. Bake at 300 degrees for 1 to 1¹/2 hours or until a wooden pick inserted in the center comes out clean. Remove to a wire rack and let cool in the pan.

Yield: 16 servings
DIAN DIAMOND

POPPY SEED CAKE

3 cups all-purpose flour
2¹/2 cups sugar
1¹/2 teaspoons baking powder
1¹/2 teaspoons salt
3 eggs
1¹/2 cups milk

1¹/2 cups vegetable oil
1¹/2 tablespoons poppy seeds
1¹/2 teaspoons vanilla extract
1¹/2 teaspoons almond extract
1¹/2 teaspoons butter flavoring

Combine the flour, sugar, baking powder, salt, eggs, milk, oil, poppy seeds, vanilla, almond extract and butter flavoring in a mixing bowl. Beat with an electric mixer at medium speed for 2 minutes. Pour the batter into 2 large or three 4×8-inch greased loaf pans. Bake at 350 degrees for 1 hour or until a wooden pick inserted in the center comes out clean. Remove to a wire rack to cool.

Yield: 2 or 3 cakes
CANDY MEYERSON

PUMPKIN PECAN BUNDT CAKE

1 (18¹/4-ounce) package spice
   cake mix
1 (4-ounce) package vanilla instant
   pudding mix
1 (16-ounce) can pumpkin
¹/2 cup vegetable oil

3 eggs
1 teaspoon cinnamon
¹/2 cup water
¹/2 cup chopped pecans
Pecan halves
Butter

Combine the cake mix, pudding mix, pumpkin, oil, eggs, cinnamon and water in a mixing bowl. Beat with an electric mixer at medium speed for 5 minutes. Add the chopped pecans and beat to mix. Arrange pecan halves in the bottom of a greased and floured bundt pan. Attach pecans halves to the side of the pan with a bit of butter. Pour in the batter. Bake at 350 degrees for 40 to 45 minutes or until a wooden pick inserted in the center comes out clean. Let cool in the pan for 10 to 15 minutes. Loosen the center and side and invert onto a wire rack to cool. Serve with whipped topping.

Yield: 16 servings
FRAN GODCHAUX

STRAWBERRY CAKE

Cake

1 (18¼-ounce) package white cake
    mix
1 (3-ounce) package strawberry
    gelatin
¼ cup all-purpose flour
4 eggs
1 cup canola oil
½ cup water
½ (10-ounce) package frozen
    sweetened strawberries, thawed

Icing

½ cup (1 stick) butter, softened
1 (16-ounce) box confectioners' sugar
½ (10-ounce) package frozen
    sweetened strawberries, thawed

For the cake, combine the cake mix, gelatin, flour, eggs, canola oil, water and strawberries in a mixing bowl. Beat until well mixed. Pour into 2 greased and floured 9-inch round cake pans. Bake at 350 degrees for 25 to 30 minutes or until a wooden pick inserted in the center comes out clean. Cool in the pans for 5 minutes. Remove to a wire rack to cool completely.

For the icing, beat the butter, confectioners' sugar and strawberries in a bowl until well mixed. Spread between the layers and over the top and side of the cooled cake. This cake may be refrigerated when assembled.

Yield: 8 servings
ALLYN HOLLADAY KRALL

My grandmother always made this cake for me on my birthday. She was not the most affectionate person, but when I arrived at her house and saw this cake (she always made it in a heart-shaped pan), I knew how much she loved me.

RUM CAKE FOR DUMMIES

1 (18¹/4-ounce) package yellow cake
    mix
1 (4-ounce) package vanilla instant
    pudding mix
¹/2 cup vegetable oil
³/4 cup water
4 eggs

¹/3 cup rum
¹/2 cup chopped nuts
¹/2 cup (1 stick) butter
1 cup sugar
¹/4 cup water
¹/4 cup rum

Combine the cake mix, pudding mix, oil, ³/4 cup water, eggs and ¹/3 cup rum in a mixing bowl. Beat with an electric mixer at medium speed for 3 minutes. Sprinkle the chopped nuts in the bottom of a greased bundt pan. Add the batter. Bake at 325 to 350 degrees for 1 hour or until a wooden pick inserted in the center comes out clean. Let cool in the pan for 10 minutes. Invert onto a serving platter. Combine the butter, sugar, ¹/4 cup water and ¹/4 cup rum in a saucepan. Bring to a boil and boil for 2 minutes. Pour over the hot cake. Serve when cool.

Yield: 10 servings
JUDGE JOHANNA FITZPATRICK

SWEDISH TEA CAKE

1/2 cup (1 stick) butter, softened
1 cup packed brown sugar
1 egg
3 egg yolks
1 teaspoon vanilla extract
1 1/2 cups cake flour

1 teaspoon baking powder
3 egg whites
1 1/2 cups packed brown sugar
1 teaspoon vanilla extract
1 cup chopped pecans

Beat the butter and 1 cup brown sugar in a bowl until light and fluffy. Beat in the egg, egg yolks and 1 teaspoon vanilla. Mix the cake flour and baking powder in a small bowl. Add to the butter mixture and beat well. Spread in an 8×10-inch cake pan. Beat the egg whites in a bowl until stiff. Fold in 1 1/2 cups brown sugar, 1 teaspoon vanilla and pecans just until mixed. Spread on top of the batter. Bake at 350 degrees for 40 minutes or until a wooden pick inserted in the center comes out clean. Remove to a wire rack to cool. Cut into squares to serve.

Yield: 6 to 8 servings
JACKIE WAITES

GRANDMA'S APPLE PIE

2 cups all-purpose flour
Pinch of salt
2 tablespoons sugar
1 1/3 teaspoons baking powder
1 cup shortening
1/4 cup orange juice
4 teaspoons vanilla extract

4 teaspoons all-purpose flour
1/2 cup sugar
Cinnamon and/or apple pie spice
    to taste
2 pounds baking apples, peeled,
    cored, sliced
1 egg, beaten

Sift 2 cups flour and the salt into a bowl. Stir in 2 tablespoons sugar and the baking powder. Cut in the shortening with a pastry blender until the consistency of small peas. Sprinkle with the orange juice and vanilla and stir just until mixed. Form into a ball. Chill, covered, until firm.

Mix 4 teaspoons flour and 1/2 cup sugar in a large bowl. Season with cinnamon. Add the apples and toss to coat. Roll out half the chilled dough on a lightly floured surface. Fit into the bottom of a 9-inch pie plate. Fill with the apple mixture. Roll out the remaining dough and fit over the top. Seal the edge and make small slits in the top of the crust to vent. Brush the crust with the beaten egg. Bake at 425 degrees for 10 minutes. Cover the edge of the crust with foil to prevent overbrowning. Reduce the oven temperature to 375 degrees and bake for 40 minutes. Remove to a wire rack to cool.

Yield: 8 servings
LAURIE MAX

My sisters and I would go to visit my grandparents frequently when we were growing up. The aroma of Grandmother Anne's apple pie was unbelievable. The crust was the best part to me due to the orange juice and vanilla! When I got married I asked her to please share this recipe with me so that I could make it—which she did a few years before she passed away.

Banana Cream Pie

1/2 cup plus 1 tablespoon sugar
1/2 cup plus 1 tablespoon
  all-purpose flour
3/4 teaspoon salt
3 cups milk, scalded
5 to 8 egg yolks, or 3 to 4 eggs
3 tablespoons butter

1/2 teaspoon vanilla extract
1 baked (9-inch) pie shell
Sliced bananas to taste
1/2 sponge cake
Apricots, cooked, mashed
Flaked coconut to taste

Combine the sugar, flour and salt in the top of a double boiler. Stir in the milk gradually. Cook over boiling water for 12 minutes. Beat the egg yolks in a bowl. Stir a small amount of the hot custard into the egg yolks. Stir the warmed egg yolks back into the custard. Stir in the butter and vanilla. Cook for 3 minutes. Pour half the custard into the pie shell. Top with a layer of bananas. Place the sponge cake layer on the bananas. Pour the remaining custard on top. Add another layer of bananas. Spread the mashed apricots over the bananas and sprinkle with coconut.

Yield: 8 servings
Judy Abroms

Judy and Hal Abroms, Jimmie Hess

FRESH BLUEBERRY PIE

As a child in New England, my whole family would go off and pick blueberries. Naturally, we came home and baked blueberry muffins and even made blueberry cordials. But the best thing was the blueberry pie.

2 cups fresh blueberries	Juice of 1 lemon
1 cup sugar	4 cups fresh blueberries
1 scant cup water	1 baked (9-inch) pie shell
1/4 cup tapioca	Whipped cream or topping

Combine 2 cups blueberries, sugar and water in a saucepan. Bring to a boil. Stir in the tapioca and lemon juice. Remove from the heat and let cool. Stir in 4 cups blueberries and pour into the pie shell. Top with whipped cream and chill until serving time.

Yield: 8 servings
JUDY ABROMS

LEMON PIE

5 egg yolks	2 (heaping) tablespoons all-purpose
1 cup sugar	flour
1 cup hot water	1 baked (9-inch) pie shell
Grated zest of 1 lemon	5 egg whites
Juice of 2 lemons	5 teaspoons confectioners' sugar

Beat the egg yolks and sugar in the top of a double boiler. Beat in the hot water, lemon zest, lemon juice and flour. Place over simmering water. Cook, stirring often, until thickened. Pour into the pie shell. Beat the egg whites in a bowl until stiff. Beat in the confectioners' sugar. Mound on top of the lemon filling. Bake at 350 degrees for 45 minutes. Remove to a wire rack to cool.

Yield: 8 servings
JOAN AND JACK BECKER

CHOCOLATE PIE

1/4 cup (1/2 stick) butter
2 cups sugar
1/4 (rounded) cup all-purpose flour
2 eggs, beaten
1 3/4 cups plus 2 tablespoons whole
  milk

1 1/2 ounces bittersweet chocolate,
  chopped
1 1/2 teaspoons vanilla extract
1 baked (9-inch) pie shell

Melt the butter in a saucepan over medium heat. Stir in the sugar and flour. Stir in the eggs and milk. Add the chocolate. Cook, stirring constantly, until thick and smooth. Remove from the heat. Stir in the vanilla. Pour into the pie shell and let cool.

Yield: 8 servings
BERNICE BARSTEIN

LEONARD'S IMPERIAL CHOCOLATE PIE

2 cups crushed chocolate sandwich
  cookies
1/4 cup (1/2 stick) margarine, melted
1/4 cup milk
1 (7-ounce) jar marshmallow creme
1 ounce semisweet chocolate, melted

1/2 teaspoon vanilla extract
1 cup whipping cream, whipped
1/4 cup slivered almonds, toasted
Chocolate sandwich cookie crumbs
  to taste

Mix 2 cups cookie crumbs and melted margarine in a bowl. Stir the milk gradually into the marshmallow creme in a bowl. Add to the cookie crumb mixture and mix. Stir in the melted chocolate and vanilla. Fold in the whipped cream and almonds. Spoon into a 9-inch pie plate. Sprinkle with additional cookie crumbs. Freeze until firm. Serve with whipped topping, if desired.

Yield: 8 servings
KAREN ALLEN

CHOCOLATE BAR PIE

1/2 cup milk
20 marshmallows
6 (1 1/2-ounce) chocolate bars with
   almonds

1 cup whipping cream
1 (9-inch) graham cracker pie shell
Vanilla wafers for garnish

Heat the milk in a saucepan to almost simmering. Stir in the marshmallows and chocolate bars. Cook over medium heat, stirring constantly, until melted. Remove from the heat and let cool. Whip the cream in a bowl. Fold into the chocolate mixture. Pour into the pie shell. Garnish with vanilla wafers and serve.

Yield: 8 servings
LAUREN PERLMAN

PEANUT BUTTER PIE

8 ounces cream cheese, softened
1 cup creamy peanut butter
1/2 (14-ounce can) sweetened
   condensed milk

1 cup whipping cream
1 (12-ounce) box vanilla wafers
1 cup peanut butter chips

Combine the cream cheese, peanut butter and sweetened condensed milk in a mixing bowl. Beat with an electric mixer until blended and smooth. Whip the cream in a bowl. Fold half the whipped cream into the peanut butter mixture. Line a 9-inch pie plate with vanilla wafers. Fill with the peanut butter mixture. Top with the remaining whipped cream and sprinkle with the peanut butter chips.

Yield: 8 servings
BARBARA WEISBERG

BUTTERMILK PECAN PIE

1/2 cup (1 stick) butter, softened
2 cups sugar
2 teaspoons vanilla extract
3 eggs
3 tablespoons all-purpose flour

1/4 teaspoon salt
1 cup buttermilk
1/2 cup chopped pecans
1 unbaked deep-dish pie shell

Beat the butter in a bowl. Beat in the sugar 1/2 cup at a time. Stir in the vanilla and eggs. Mix the flour and salt in a bowl. Stir in the dry ingredients gradually. Add the buttermilk and mix well. Sprinkle the chopped pecans in the bottom of the pie shell. Pour the filling over the pecans. Bake at 300 degrees for 1 hour and 30 minutes or until set. Remove to a wire rack and let cool to room temperature.

Yield: 6 to 8 servings
LINDA APPLEBAUM

SOUTHERN PECAN PIE

3 eggs, beaten
1/2 cup sugar
1/4 teaspoon salt
2 tablespoons all-purpose flour
1 cup Golden Eagle table syrup

2 teaspoons vanilla extract
1/4 cup (1/2 stick) margarine, melted
1 cup small pecan pieces
1 unbaked (9-inch) pie shell

Mix the eggs, sugar, salt, flour, syrup, vanilla and melted margarine in a bowl. Sprinkle the pecan pieces in the bottom of the pie shell. Add the filling. Cover the edge of the crust with foil to prevent overbrowning. Bake at 375 degrees for 10 to 12 minutes. Reduce the oven temperature to 325 degrees and bake for 25 to 30 minutes longer or until the center is set.

Yield: 8 servings
DENISE LEWIS

GERMAN BUTTER COOKIES

When I was teaching school at an Army base in Fort Knox, Kentucky (about 1972), there was a German student in my class whose mother was an incredible cook. She made these wonderfully delicious cookies for our class parties and I eventually talked her into giving me the recipe.

3 cups all-purpose flour	1 cup (2 sticks) margarine, softened
1 cup sugar	2 eggs
1 package vanillin sugar	1 teaspoon rum
1/4 teaspoon cinnamon	

Mound the flour, sugar, vanillin sugar and cinnamon on a work surface. Make a hole in the center and add the margarine, eggs and rum. Mix with hands to form a dough. Roll out on a lightly floured surface to 1/4-inch thickness. Cut with a cookie cutter and decorate, if desired. Place on an ungreased cookie sheet. Bake at 350 degrees until lightly browned. Remove cookies to a wire rack to cool.

Note: The dough may be mixed in a large bowl with a wooden spoon, if desired.

Yield: 3 to 4 dozen cookies
LAURIE MAX

DUTCH BUTTER COOKIES

3/4 cup (1 1/2 sticks) butter, softened	1 cup all-purpose flour
2/3 cup sugar	1 (scant) cup whole wheat flour
1 egg white	1 egg yolk
1/2 teaspoon vanilla extract	Milk, sugar and cinnmon to taste

Beat the butter, 2/3 cup sugar, egg white and vanilla in a bowl. Stir in the all-purpose flour and whole wheat flour and mix well. Spread the dough evenly on a greased cookie sheet. Mix the egg yolk with a small amount of milk in a bowl and brush over the dough. Sprinkle generously with sugar to taste and cinnamon. Bake at 375 degrees for 10 to 15 minutes or until golden brown. Cool on the cookie sheet slightly. Cut into squares to serve.

Yield: 2 to 3 dozen cookies
CANTOR JESSICA ROSKIN

AUNTIE ANN'S CINNAMON SWIRL COOKIES

4 cups all-purpose flour
4 (heaping) teaspoons baking powder
1 (heaping) teaspoon salt
4 (heaping) tablespoons sugar
4 eggs
5 tablespoons plus 1 teaspoon
   vegetable oil

1/2 cup milk
1 teaspoon vanilla extract
Vegetable oil for brushing
1 cup finely chopped nuts
Sugar to taste
Cinnamon to taste

Sift the flour, baking powder and salt into a bowl. Beat 4 tablespoons sugar, eggs and 5 tablespoons plus 1 teaspoon oil in a large bowl. Beat in the dry ingredients alternately with the milk. Stir in the vanilla. Chill the dough, covered, for several hours or overnight. Roll out 1/4 of the dough on a lightly floured surface to a 1/4-inch-thick rectangle. Brush with additional oil. Sprinkle with 1/4 of the nuts, sugar to taste and cinnamon. Roll up lengthwise and cut into slices with a knife dipped in flour. Repeat with the remaining dough and filling. Place on a greased cookie sheet. Bake at 375 degrees until golden brown. Remove cookies to a wire rack to cool. Can be frozen when cool.

Yield: 16 to 17 dozen cookies
ANITA MAY

Anita and Bob May and their children, Harvey, Ann, and Julie and their families.

ICE CREAM STRUDEL

1 cup vanilla ice cream	1/2 cup chopped nuts
1 cup (2 sticks) butter, melted	1/4 cup chopped dried apricots or
2 cups all-purpose flour	raisins
1 cup apricot preserves	1 tablespoon milk

Combine the ice cream and melted butter in a food processor. Process until mixed. Add the flour and process until the mixture forms a dough. Divide into 4 balls. Chill for 1 hour. Roll out 1 ball of dough on a lightly floured surface to a rectangle. Spread with 1/4 of the preserves. Sprinkle with 1/4 of the nuts and apricots. Roll up lengthwise. Repeat with the remaining dough and filling. Place on a baking sheet. Brush with the milk. Bake at 350 degrees for 45 minutes. Slice when cool.

Yield: 8 servings
JOANNA GOTLIEB

CHOCOLATE LACE COOKIES

3/4 cup (1 1/2 sticks) butter	3 3/4 cups chopped nuts
6 ounces packed brown sugar	4 cups semisweet chocolate chips,
3 tablespoons Lyles Golden Syrup	melted
1 1/2 cups self-rising flour	

Combine the butter, brown sugar and syrup in a saucepan. Heat until the sugar dissolves, stirring constantly. Remove from the heat. Mix the self-rising flour and nuts in a bowl. Add the hot syrup mixture and mix well. Place small spoonfuls of cookie batter on a foil-lined cookie sheet. Bake at 325 degrees for 10 to 15 minutes. Remove the cookies to a wire rack to cool. Coat the smooth side of each cookie with the melted chocolate. Let the chocolate cool and harden. Store the cookies in a covered tin.

Yield: 6 to 8 dozen cookies
JOYCE HELZBERG

CORNFLAKE COOKIES

2 egg whites
1 cup sugar
2 cups cornflakes

1/2 teaspoon salt
1/2 teaspoon vanilla extract
1 cup chopped nuts

Beat the egg whites in a bowl until stiff. Add the sugar and gently mix. Fold in the cornflakes, salt, vanilla and nuts. Drop by teaspoonfuls onto a greased cookie sheet. Bake at 350 degrees until golden brown. Remove the cookies to a wire rack to cool.

Yield: 2 to 3 dozen cookies
DODIE JAFFE AND JUDY BORISKY

ANNIE ABELSON'S FINGER COOKIES

1/2 cup (1 stick) butter, softened
3 tablespoons confectioners' sugar
1 cup finely chopped nuts
3 tablespoons cold water

1 teaspoon vanilla extract
1 1/2 cups all-purpose flour
Confectioners' sugar to taste

Beat the butter and 3 tablespoons confectioners' sugar in a bowl until light and fluffy. Stir in the nuts, cold water and vanilla. Add the flour and mix well. Roll the dough into marble-size balls. Roll the balls on a work surface to elongate them. Arrange on an ungreased cookie sheet. Bake at 300 degrees for 30 minutes or until lightly browned. Roll the hot cookies in confectioners' sugar to taste and place on a wire rack to cool. Roll in confectioners' sugar again when the cookies are cool.

Yield: 3 to 4 dozen cookies
ROSALYN SIEGAL

JELLY COOKIES

1 1/2 cups (3 sticks) butter or margarine, softened	1 teaspoon vanilla extract
1 cup sugar	1/2 teaspoon salt
3 egg yolks	4 cups all-purpose flour
	Currant jelly (or a favorite flavor)

Beat the butter and sugar in a large bowl until light and fluffy. Beat in the egg yolks, vanilla and salt. Beat in the flour. Roll the dough into small balls and place on a cookie sheet. Make an indentation in the center of each ball and fill with currant jelly. Bake at 350 degrees for 8 to 10 minutes or until lightly browned. Remove cookies to a wire rack to cool.

Yield: (about) 8 dozen cookies

LEE UNGER LICHTER

SURPRISE MERINGUE COOKIES

2 egg whites, at room temperature	3/4 cup sugar
1/8 teaspoon salt	1 cup semisweet chocolate chips
1/8 teaspoon cream of tartar	1/3 cup chopped walnuts (optional)
1 scant teaspoon vanilla extract	

Combine the egg whites, salt, cream of tartar and vanilla in a bowl. Beat until soft peaks form. Add the sugar gradually and continue beating until stiff peaks form. Fold in the chocolate chips and walnuts. Drop the mixture by rounded teaspoonfuls onto a cookie sheet lined with plain brown paper. Bake at 300 degrees for 25 minutes. Remove cookies to a wire rack to cool.

Yield: 6 to 7 dozen cookies

SUSAN K. BIEDINGER

PRESIDENTIAL COOKIES

2 cups (4 sticks) butter, softened
1 cup sugar
4 cups sifted all-purpose flour
1/2 teaspoon salt

2 teaspoons vanilla extract
2 cups chopped pecans
Confectioners' sugar

Beat the butter and sugar in a large bowl until light and fluffy. Beat in the flour, salt, vanilla and pecans. Roll the dough into small balls and place on a cookie sheet. Press each ball with a fork to flatten. Bake at 350 degrees for about 12 minutes. Remove the cookies to a wire rack to cool. Sprinkle with confectioners' sugar when cool.

Yield: (about) 8 dozen cookies
LOUISE LEVIN

SUGAR COOKIES

1 1/2 cups confectioners' sugar
1 cup (2 sticks) butter or margarine,
  softened
1 teaspoon vanilla extract
1/2 teaspoon almond extract

1 egg
2 1/2 cups all-purpose flour
1 teaspoon baking powder
1 teaspoon cream of tartar
Sugar

Mix the confectioners' sugar, butter, vanilla, almond extract and egg in a bowl until well blended. Stir in the flour, baking powder and cream of tartar and mix well. Chill, covered, for 3 hours. Divide the dough in half. Roll each half 3/16 inch thick on a lightly floured surface. Cut into desired shapes and sprinkle with sugar. Place on a lightly greased (or parchment paper-lined) cookie sheet. Bake at 375 degrees for 7 to 8 minutes or until the edges are golden brown.

Yield: (about) 5 dozen cookies
ELLEN DORSKY

PINK PARTY COOKIES

Cookies

3/4 cup (1 1/2 sticks) butter,
   softened
1/4 cup shortening
1/2 cup confectioners' sugar
2 cups sifted all-purpose flour
1/2 teaspoon vanilla extract

Frosting

1 (16-ounce) box confectioners' sugar
1/2 cup (1 stick) butter or margarine,
   softened
1 teaspoon vanilla extract
3 to 4 tablespoons milk
Drop of red food coloring

For the cookies, beat the butter, shortening and confectioners' sugar in a bowl until light and fluffy. Add the flour and vanilla and mix well. Let stand for 30 minutes. Roll the dough into small balls and arrange on a cookie sheet. Flatten each ball with a fork dipped in flour to make a crisscross pattern. Bake at 325 degrees until the edges are lightly browned. Remove the cookies to a wire rack to cool.

For the frosting, combine the confectioners' sugar, butter, vanilla, milk and food coloring in a mixing bowl. Beat with an electric mixer at medium speed for 1 to 2 minutes or until smooth. Spread a layer of frosting over half the cookies. Top with the remaining cookies to make sandwiches.

Yield: 2 to 3 dozen sandwich cookies
JULIE LEVINSON-GABIS

FRED'S FAMOUS REDUCED-FAT OATMEAL RAISIN COOKIES

If you like delicately crispy, thin cookies, stop reading right now. That's not what this recipe is AT ALL. These cookies are mini-cakes, tall, hearty, tough, doughy, like New Jersey. I evolved this recipe over many years from Quaker's Vanishing Oatmeal Raisin Cookie recipe. This is my second most-requested recipe.

1 cup packed brown sugar	*1 teaspoon baking soda*
1/2 cup sugar	*1 teaspoon cinnamon*
1/2 cup applesauce	*1/2 teaspoon salt*
1/2 cup safflower oil	*1 1/2 cups all-purpose flour*
1/2 cup egg substitute	*3 cups rolled oats*
1 teaspoon vanilla extract	*1 cup raisins*

Beat the brown sugar, sugar, applesauce and safflower oil in a large bowl. Beat in the egg substitute and vanilla. Add the baking soda, cinnamon and salt and mix well. Stir in the flour and oats gradually. Fold in the raisins. Drop by 1/8 to 1/4 cupfuls onto an ungreased cookie sheet. Bake at 350 degrees for 12 to 15 minutes or until the tops start to brown. Underbake rather than overbake. Let cool for 1 minute on the cookie sheet. Remove to a wire rack to cool.

Yield: (about) 20 cookies

FREDERICK KAIMANN

"TO DIE FOR" COOKIES

1 cup (2 sticks) butter, softened
1 cup sugar
1 cup packed brown sugar
1 egg
1 cup vegetable oil
1 cup rolled oats
1 cup crushed cornflakes

1/2 cup flaked coconut
1 cup chopped pecans
1 teaspoon vanilla extract
3 1/2 cups all-purpose flour
1 teaspoon baking soda
1 teaspoon salt

Beat the butter, sugar, brown sugar, egg and oil in a bowl until well mixed. Stir in the oats, cornflakes, coconut, pecans and vanilla. Mix the flour, baking soda and salt in a bowl. Stir into the cornflake mixture. Roll the dough into small balls and place on an ungreased cookie sheet. Flatten each ball with a fork dipped in water. Bake at 325 degrees for 12 minutes. Let cool on the cookie sheet.

Yield: 5 dozen cookies
JEAN SKLAR

THE WORLD'S BEST BROWNIES

4 ounces bittersweet chocolate
1 cup (2 sticks) butter
4 eggs
2 cups sugar
1 1/3 cups cake flour

1 teaspoon baking powder
1/2 teaspoon salt
2 cups semisweet chocolate chips
1 teaspoon vanilla extract
1/2 cup chopped pecans or walnuts

Melt the chocolate and butter in the top of a double boiler over simmering water. Remove from the heat and chill. Beat the eggs in a bowl with an electric mixer. Beat in the sugar gradually. Beat in the chilled chocolate mixture. Sift the cake flour, baking powder and salt into a bowl. Beat gradually into the chocolate mixture. Stir in the chocolate chips and vanilla. Pour the batter into a greased and floured 9×13-inch baking dish. Sprinkle with the pecans. Bake at 350 degrees for 20 minutes or until a wooden pick inserted in the center comes out clean. Remove to a wire rack to cool. Cut when ready to serve. Keep tightly covered.

Yield: 2 dozen brownies
BUNNY ROTENSTREICH

GRANDMA BRESLER BROWNIES

3 ounces unsweetened chocolate
1 cup (2 sticks) margarine
4 eggs
2 cups sugar

1 cup sifted all-purpose flour
1 cup pecan pieces
1 teaspoon vanilla extract

Melt the unsweetened chocolate and margarine in the top of a double boiler over simmering water. Remove from the heat and let cool. Beat the eggs in a bowl until pale yellow. Beat in the sugar and cooled chocolate mixture. Stir in the flour, pecans and vanilla. Pour the batter into a greased 9-inch square cake pan. Bake at 325 degrees for 35 to 45 minutes or until a wooden pick inserted in the center comes out clean. Remove to a wire rack and cut into squares when cool.

Yield: (about) 16 brownies
SALLIE KARTUS DOWNS

This is "THE RECIPE" that my grandmother, Helene Bresler, was known for, and will be remembered for, for generations to come. I "talk" to my grandma every time I make them—I wonder what it felt like to be her when she was in her kitchen baking brownies that caused so much excitement among her family. I feel a closeness, a connection to my grandmother— because she shared her "secret recipe" with me. I asked her what was the secret to making the best brownies in the world and she said, "you just throw it all together." The brownies had a great consistency—the top was crispy and crumbly and the body was moist. My grandmother and I had a very special relationship—she nurtured me, supported me, encouraged me, and is today one of my greatest mentors. I struggled with whether I should share this recipe, because it is so personal and sacred, but now that grandma is in heaven, I know she would want to share the recipe. No one will ever make them as good as grandma.

Sallie Downs and Helene Bresler

MOM'S BROWNIES

2 eggs
1 cup sugar
1/2 teaspoon vanilla extract
2 1/2 ounces unsweetened chocolate
1/3 cup shortening

1/2 cup all-purpose flour
1/2 teaspoon baking powder
1/8 teaspoon salt
1 cup pecan pieces (optional)

Beat the eggs in a bowl until pale yellow. Beat in the sugar and gradually stir in the vanilla. Melt the unsweetened chocolate and shortening in the top of a double boiler over simmering water. Add the melted chocolate to the egg mixture and mix well. Sift the flour, baking powder and salt into a bowl. Add to the chocolate mixture and mix well. Add the pecans and stir to mix. Spread in a greased 9-inch square cake pan. Bake at 325 degrees for 30 minutes or until the brownies pull away from the sides of the pan. Remove to a wire rack to cool. Cut into squares while hot. Let cool before removing brownies from the pan.

Yield: (about) 16 brownies
ETHEL FLEISHER

BASIC BROWNIES

3/4 cup (1 1/2 sticks) butter, melted
1 1/2 cups sugar
1 1/2 teaspoons vanilla extract
3 eggs

3/4 cup all-purpose flour
1/2 cup baking cocoa
1/2 teaspoon baking powder
1/2 teaspoon salt

Mix the melted butter, sugar and vanilla in a bowl. Add the eggs and beat well with a spoon. Mix the flour, baking cocoa, baking powder and salt in a bowl. Stir into the egg mixture gradually and mix well. Spread in a greased 8-inch square cake pan. Bake at 350 degrees for 40 to 45 minutes or until the brownies pull away from the sides of the pan. Remove to a wire rack and cut into squares when cool.

Yield: 16 brownies
CELESTE FLEISHER

BROWNIES

2 ounces unsweetened chocolate
1/2 cup (1 stick) margarine
1 cup sugar
1/2 cup all-purpose flour

2 eggs, lightly beaten
3/4 cup pecan pieces
1 teaspoon instant coffee crystals
1 teaspoon vanilla extract

Melt the chocolate and margarine in a microwave-safe bowl in the microwave. Stir in the sugar. Stir in the flour. Add the eggs and mix well. Stir in the pecans, coffee crystals and vanilla. Spread in an 8-inch square cake pan coated with baking spray. Bake at 325 degrees for 25 minutes or until the brownies pull away from the sides of the pan. Remove to a wire rack and cut when cool.

Yield: 16 brownies
NORMA WARREN

NELLE'S BUTTERSCOTCH BROWNIES

1/3 cup butter
1 cup packed dark brown sugar
1 egg
3/4 cup all-purpose flour
1/4 teaspoon salt

1/2 teaspoon baking powder
1 teaspoon vanilla extract
1/2 cup chopped nuts
Confectioners' sugar (optional)

Cook the butter and brown sugar in a saucepan until bubbly and caramelized. Remove from the heat and let cool. Combine the cooled butter mixture, egg, flour, salt, baking powder, vanilla and nuts in a bowl and mix well. Pour into a greased 8-inch square cake pan lined with waxed paper. Bake at 325 degrees for 30 minutes or until the brownies pull away from the sides of the pan. Let cool in the pan for 5 minutes. Invert onto a cutting board and cut into squares. Dust with confectioners' sugar.

Yield: 16 brownies
PAT WEIL

CHESS PIE SQUARES

1 (18¼-ounce) package yellow
    cake mix
½ cup (1 stick) butter or margarine,
    melted
1 egg

1 (16-ounce) box confectioners'
    sugar, sifted
3 eggs
8 ounces cream cheese, softened
1 teaspoon vanilla extract

Combine the cake mix, melted butter and 1 egg in a mixing bowl. Beat with
an electric mixer at medium speed until well blended. Press the dough into a
greased and floured 9×13-inch cake pan. Combine the confectioners' sugar,
3 eggs, cream cheese and vanilla in a mixing bowl. Beat with an electric mixer
at medium speed until smooth. Pour over the dough in the cake pan. Bake
at 350 degrees for 35 to 40 minutes or until a wooden pick inserted in the
center comes out clean. Remove to a wire rack and let cool until warm, not
completely cooled. Cut into squares and remove from the pan.

Yield: 2 to 3 dozen squares
MOLLIE GOTTLIEB

KATE'S TOFFEE BARS

½ cup shortening
½ cup (1 stick) butter, softened
1 cup packed brown sugar
1 egg

1 teaspoon vanilla extract
2¼ cups all-purpose flour
2 cups semisweet chocolate chips
Ground pecans or walnuts

Beat the shortening, butter, and brown sugar in a bowl until fluffy. Beat in the
egg and vanilla. Stir in the flour and mix well. Spread the dough evenly on a
12×17-inch baking sheet. Bake at 350 degrees for 20 to 25 minutes. Remove
from the oven and sprinkle with the chocolate chips. Return to the oven for
a few minutes. Remove and spread the melted chocolate evenly over the top.
Sprinkle with the pecans. Cut into squares immediately. Let cool before
removing from the baking sheet. Chill in the freezer for a few minutes if the
chocolate is not firm. Store in an airtight container with waxed paper between
the layers of bars. Freezes well.

Yield: (about) 6 dozen
MRS. KATE MALKOVE

AUNT TESSIE'S MARBLE SQUARES

Cheese Filling
96 ounces cream cheese, softened
1/2 cup (1 stick) butter or margarine,
    softened
3 cups sugar
1/4 cup cornstarch
2 teaspoons vanilla extract
10 eggs
2 cups sour cream

Chocolate Layer
4 cups (8 sticks) margarine, softened
10 cups sugar
24 eggs
4 teaspoons vanilla extract
1 teaspoon almond flavoring
5 cups semisweet chocolate chips
1 cup (2 sticks) butter
1 tablespoon baking powder
6 to 7 cups all-purpose flour
Chopped nuts (optional)

For the cheese filling, beat the cream cheese, butter, sugar, cornstarch, vanilla, eggs and sour cream in a very large bowl until smooth.

For the chocolate layer, beat the margarine and sugar in a very large bowl until light and fluffy. Beat in the eggs, vanilla and almond flavoring. Melt the chocolate chips and butter in the top of a large double boiler over simmering water. Add the melted chocolate to the egg mixture and mix well. Beat in the baking powder and flour. Stir in nuts. Reserve about 1/3 of the mixture and divide the remaining batter between 4 large greased baking pans. Top with the cheese filling. Drop spoonfuls of the reserved chocolate mixture over the cream cheese layer. Swirl with a knife to create a marbleized effect. Bake at 350 degrees for 35 minutes or until a wooden pick inserted in the center comes out a little moist. Cut into squares when cool.

Yield: (about) 20 dozen squares
LYNNE AND MARK COHEN
from TESSIE COHEN

Aunt Tessie's original recipes could feed an entire city... and did through Felix's Delicatessen on 4th Avenue North and 18th Street, owned and operated by Uncle Felix and Aunt Tessie Cohen. As children, my mother and daddy would take all six of us to Felix's where, with sawdust on the floor and salamis drying on hooks, we'd peer into the pickle barrels, walk with amazement down the aisles of groceries and fresh beautiful produce selected by Uncle Felix at the farmer's market each morning before dawn, look at cans of strange and wonderful delicacies, have questions about all the jars of colorful homemade pickled vegetables and preserved fruits, ask for tastes of halavah (which we'd get if we were good), and eat delicious corned beef or pastrami sandwiches (at a time when all the meats were marinated and cooked in the store). There was always a wonderful aroma around their grocery/deli.

DESSERT ROLLS

4 cups all-purpose flour
1 tablespoon baking powder
2 cups (4 sticks) butter, softened

16 ounces cream cheese, softened
Fruit filling of your choice
Confectioners' sugar

Combine the flour and baking powder in a large bowl. Cut in the butter and cream cheese with a pastry blender. Knead to form a smooth elastic dough. Chill, covered, until firm. Roll out circles of dough on a lightly floured surface. Cut into wedges. Spoon fruit filling at the wide end of the wedges and roll up. Place on a baking sheet. Bake at 350 degrees for 15 to 20 minutes. Remove the rolls to a wire rack to cool. Dust with confectioners' sugar when cool.

Yield: 2 dozen rolls
BELLA IMAS

*Maria Grigoryev,
Alexi Grigoryev and
Bella Imas*

LEMON SOUFFLÉ

2 envelopes unflavored gelatin
1/2 cup water
6 eggs
1 1/2 cups sugar

1 tablespoon grated lemon zest
Juice of 4 lemons
1 1/2 cups whipping cream

Sprinkle the gelatin over the water in a small saucepan. Let stand for 10 minutes. Cook over low heat until dissolved and clear. Remove from the heat and let cool. Combine the eggs and sugar in a mixing bowl. Beat at high speed with an electric mixer for 7 to 8 minutes or until thick and light. Stir the lemon zest and lemon juice into the cooled gelatin mixture. Add to the egg mixture and beat until blended. Remove the bowl from the mixer and chill for 5 minutes. Beat the whipping cream in a bowl until soft peaks form. Fold into the lemon mixture until no white streaks are visible. Spoon into a 1 1/2-quart soufflé dish and chill until set.

Yield: 8 servings
NANCY GOEDECKE

GREAT LIGHT BANANA PUDDING

1 (12-ounce) container light
    whipped topping
1 (14-ounce) can fat-free sweetened
    condensed milk
1 (4-ounce) package vanilla instant
    pudding mix

1 1/2 cups skim milk
1 (12-ounce) package reduced-fat
    vanilla wafers
6 to 7 ripe bananas, sliced

Combine the whipped topping, sweetened condensed milk, pudding mix and skim milk in a mixing bowl. Beat with an electric mixer at low speed for 5 minutes. Line the bottom of a large trifle bowl with a layer of vanilla wafers. Top with a layer of bananas. Pour a layer of pudding mixture over the top. Repeat layers until all ingredients are used. Chill, covered, until ready to serve.

Note: You may reserve 2 ounces of the whipped topping to garnish the top of the trifle.

Yield: 8 servings
JAMIE AND GREG ODREZIN

STRAWBERRY AND PRETZEL CRUST GELATIN

1¹/2 cups crushed pretzels
¹/2 cup sugar
¹/2 cup (1 stick) margarine, melted
8 ounces cream cheese, softened
1 (8-ounce) container whipped
    topping
¹/2 cup confectioners' sugar

1 (6-ounce) package strawberry
    gelatin
2 cups boiling water
1 (20-ounce) can crushed pineapple,
    drained
1 (10-ounce) package frozen
    sweetened sliced strawberries

Mix the pretzels, sugar and melted margarine in a bowl. Press into the bottom of a 9×13-inch baking dish. Bake at 350 degrees for 10 minutes. Remove to a wire rack to cool. Beat the cream cheese, whipped topping and confectioners' sugar in a bowl until well blended. Spread on top of the cooled crust. Chill until cold. Combine the gelatin and boiling water in a bowl. Stir to dissolve gelatin. Add the pineapple and frozen strawberries. Stir until the strawberries thaw and break apart. Spoon gently over the cream cheese layer. Chill, covered, until set.

Yield: 12 servings
SUSAN BARSTEIN

Susan Barstein and grandmother

Pudding

1 loaf French bread
4 cups milk
3 eggs
2 cups sugar
2 tablespoons vanilla extract
1 cup raisins
3 tablespoons margarine, melted

Whiskey Sauce

1 cup sugar
1 egg
1/2 cup (1 stick) margarine, melted
Whiskey to taste

For the pudding, soak the bread in the milk in a bowl. Mix with hands until well combined. Stir in the eggs, sugar, vanilla and raisins. Pour the melted margarine into a 9×13-inch baking pan and tilt to coat the bottom. Pour in the pudding mixture. Bake at 325 degrees until very firm. Remove to a wire rack to cool. Cut into squares when cool.

For the whiskey sauce, beat the sugar and egg in a bowl until well mixed. Add the melted margarine and stir until the sugar dissolves. Add whiskey and stir until smooth. Place pudding on heatproof serving plates. Top with whiskey sauce and heat under the broiler.

Yield: 9 to 12 servings
MARGOT MARX

George's Challah Bread Pudding

1 large challah, cut into cubes
2 pears, peeled, cored, chopped
2 apples, peeled, cored, chopped
1 1/4 cup raisins
1/2 cup sweetened dried cranberries
1 (2-ounce) package sliced almonds
1/2 cup sugar
1 1/2 teaspoons cinnamon
1 teaspoon allspice
1/2 teaspoon nutmeg

1/2 teaspoon salt
3 eggs, beaten
1 (14-ounce) can sweetened
  condensed milk
1 (12-ounce) can evaporated milk
1 teaspoon vanilla extract
2 tablespoons rum
1/2 cup (1 stick) butter or margarine,
  melted

Mix the challah, pears, apples, raisins, dried cranberries and almonds in a large bowl. Mix the sugar, cinnamon, allspice, nutmeg and salt in a small bowl. Add to the bread mixture and toss to coat. Stir the eggs, sweetened condensed milk, evaporated milk, vanilla, rum and melted butter in a bowl. Pour over the bread mixture and stir until well mixed. Pour into a large baking dish and press down with a spoon. Bake at 350 degrees for 2 hours or until firm and golden brown.

Yield: 12 servings
GEORGE THOMPSON

Apple Pay

3 apples, peeled, cored, chopped
5 eggs
1 cup sugar

1 cup all-purpose flour
1 teaspoon vanilla extract

Arrange the apples in a well-buttered baking dish. Beat the eggs in a bowl with an electric mixer until pale yellow. Add the sugar, flour and vanilla. Beat until well mixed. Pour the batter over the apples. Bake at 350 degrees for 45 minutes. Remove to a wire rack to cool. Invert onto a serving plate when cool.

Yield: 6 servings
BELLA IMAS

ALMOND TOSCA BAKED APPLE

1/2 cup (1 stick) unsalted butter
6 tablespoons sugar
2 tablespoons heavy cream
2 tablespoons all-purpose flour
2 egg yolks

1 whole vanilla bean, split
3/4 cup slivered almonds
1 (or more) baking apple per guest
Whipped cream to taste
Sliced or slivered almonds to taste

Melt the butter in the top of a double boiler over simmering water. Stir in the sugar, cream, flour, egg yolks and vanilla bean. Cook, stirring constantly, until thickened. Remove from the heat and remove the vanilla bean. Stir in the slivered almonds. Peel and core the apples. Place in a buttered baking dish. Spoon the vanilla sauce over the apples and into the cores. Bake at 375 degrees for 15 to 20 minutes. Serve topped with whipped cream and sliced almonds.

Yield: variable
PAT SAUL

BLUEBERRY CRUNCH

1 (20-ounce) can crushed pineapple
3 cups blueberries
3/4 cup sugar
1 (18 1/4-ounce) package yellow
    cake mix

1/2 cup (1 stick) margarine, melted
1/4 cup sugar
1 cup chopped pecans

Spread the undrained pineapple in the bottom of a buttered 9x13-inch baking dish. Mix the blueberries with 3/4 cup sugar in a bowl. Sprinkle over the pineapple. Spread the cake mix over the fruit and drizzle with the melted margarine. Sprinkle 1/4 cup sugar and the pecans over the top. Bake at 350 degrees for 40 minutes or until a wooden pick inserted in the center comes out clean. Remove to a wire rack to cool.

Yield: 12 servings
KAREN ALLEN

CHOCOLATE PIZZA

14 ounces dark chocolate bark
8 ounces white chocolate bark
1¹/2 cups crisp rice cereal
1 cup (or more) peanuts

2 cups miniature marshmallows
"M&M's" Chocolate Candies
2 ounces white chocolate bark
1 teaspoon (or more) vegetable oil

Place the dark chocolate and 8 ounces white chocolate in a microwave-safe bowl coated with nonstick cooking spray. Microwave on Low until melted. Stir in the cereal, peanuts and marshmallows. Spread in a pizza pan coated with nonstick cooking spray. Push with a spoon to flatten. Sprinkle the surface with the candies. Combine 2 ounces white chocolate and the oil in a small microwave-safe bowl. Microwave on Low until melted. Drizzle over the top of the pizza. Chill, if desired, but do not freeze.

Yield: 16 servings
LOIS M. COHEN

Lots of people have the recipe that I call Miss Lois' chocolate pizza. But several of the children have asked that I submit my recipe for consideration for the From Generation to Generation *cookbook. I first saw this fabulous chocoholic's dream at Jennifer Goldstein's Bat Mitzvah. I asked you about it and you said it was so easy to make. Not being a "cook," I could not believe that something so delicious looking was truly easy. But it really is! And such a crowd pleaser!*

1 cup sifted all-purpose flour	*1/4 teaspoon salt*
1/4 cup sugar	*5 eggs*
1 teaspoon grated lemon zest	*2 egg yolks*
1/2 cup (1 stick) butter or margarine	*1/4 cup heavy cream*
1 egg yolk, beaten	*1 cup strawberries, crushed*
1/4 teaspoon vanilla extract	*1 cup water*
40 ounces cream cheese, softened	*1 1/2 teaspoons cornstarch*
1/4 teaspoon vanilla extract	*1/2 to 3/4 cup sugar*
3/4 teaspoon grated lemon zest	*Red food coloring (optional)*
1 3/4 cups sugar	*1 to 2 cups whole strawberries*
3 tablespoons all-purpose flour	*Canned pineapple rings, halved*

Mix 1 cup flour, 1/4 cup sugar and 1 teaspoon lemon zest in a bowl. Cut in the butter until crumbly. Add 1 egg yolk and 1/4 teaspoon vanilla and mix well. Remove the side from a 9-inch springform pan. Pat 1/3 of the dough evenly over the bottom of the pan. Bake at 400 degrees for 6 minutes or until golden brown. Remove to a wire rack and let cool. Butter the side of the pan and attach carefully to the bottom. Pat the remaining dough 2 inches up the side of the pan.

Beat the cream cheese until fluffy. Beat in 1/4 teaspoon vanilla and 3/4 teaspoon lemon zest. Mix 1 3/4 cups sugar, 3 tablespoons flour and salt in a bowl. Beat into the cream cheese mixture gradually. Add the eggs and 2 egg yolks 1 at a time, beating well after each addition. Stir in the cream gently. Pour into the springform pan. Bake at 500 degrees for 5 to 8 minutes or until the top edge of the crust is golden brown. Reduce the oven temperature to 200 degrees and bake for 1 hour. Remove to a wire rack and let cool in the pan for about 3 hours. Place the cheesecake on a large plate. Loosen from the side of the pan with a sharp knife and remove the side of the pan.

Combine 1 cup crushed strawberries and water in a saucepan. Cook for 2 minutes. Strain through a sieve and discard the solids. Return the strained liquid to the saucepan. Mix the cornstarch and 1/2 cup sugar in a bowl. Add to the saucepan and stir to mix. Bring to a boil, stirring constantly. Cook, stirring constantly, until thick and clear. Remove from the heat and add a few drops of red food coloring. Let cool to room temperature. Arrange 1 to 2 cups whole strawberries on top of the cooled cheesecake. Surround the strawberries with the pineapple halves. Pour the glaze on top. Chill for about 2 hours.

Yield: 10 servings
PATSY COLLAT

GLORIA HOWTON'S CHEESECAKE

24 ounces cream cheese,
   softened
1¼ cups sugar
4 eggs
1 teaspoon vanilla extract

Graham cracker crust pressed into a
   9-inch springform pan
2 cups sour cream
¼ cup sugar
1 teaspoon vanilla extract

Combine the cream cheese, 1¼ cups sugar, eggs and 1 teaspoon vanilla in a mixing bowl. Beat with an electric mixer at medium speed for 25 minutes. Pour into the prepared crust. Bake at 350 degrees for 30 minutes. Remove from the oven. Stir the sour cream, ¼ cup sugar and 1 teaspoon vanilla in a bowl. Spread over the top of the hot cheesecake. Bake for 10 minutes longer. Remove to a wire rack to cool. Chill until cold. Place the cheesecake on a large plate. Loosen from the side of the pan with a sharp knife and remove the side of the pan.

Yield: 8 to 10 servings
GLORIA HOWTON

FROZEN PEANUT BUTTER CHEESECAKE

24 ounces cream cheese, softened
1 (14-ounce) can sweetened
   condensed milk
3 cups creamy peanut butter
2 teaspoons vanilla extract

1 cup whipping cream
1 (12-ounce) box vanilla wafers
2 cups whipping cream
1 teaspoon vanilla extract
Peanut butter chips (optional)

Combine the cream cheese, sweetened condensed milk, peanut butter and 2 teaspoons vanilla in a mixing bowl. Beat with an electric mixer until well blended. Beat 1 cup whipping cream in a bowl and fold gently into the peanut butter mixture. Line the bottom of a springform pan with vanilla wafers. Pour the batter into the pan. Arrange the remaining vanilla wafers against the side of the pan. Beat 2 cups whipping cream and 1 teaspoon vanilla in a bowl. Spread over the top of the cheesecake. Sprinkle with peanut butter chips. Freeze for 3 to 4 hours. Let thaw at room temperature for 1 to 1½ hours and serve immediately.

Yield: 10 servings
BARBARA DEE WEISBERG

MAMMA'S CHEESECAKE

1 package graham cracker crumbs
1/2 cup (1 stick) butter, melted
1/2 cup sugar
1 teaspoon cinnamon
24 ounces cream cheese, softened
2 cups sour cream

2 scant cups sugar
2 tablespoons all-purpose flour
6 eggs, at room temperature
Grated zest of 1 1/2 lemons
Juice of 1 1/2 lemons
1 teaspoon vanilla extract

Combine the graham cracker crumbs, melted butter, 1/2 cup sugar and the cinnamon in a bowl. Stir until well mixed. Press into the bottom and up the side of a greased 8-inch springform pan, reserving some for topping. Beat the cream cheese in a bowl with an electric mixer until fluffy. Beat in the sour cream. Mix 2 cups sugar and the flour in a bowl. Beat into the cream cheese mixture gradually. Add the eggs 1 at a time, beating well after each addition. Beat in the lemon zest, lemon juice and vanilla. Pour into the prepared crust. Sprinkle the reserved crumbs over the top. Bake at 350 degrees for 1 hour. Turn off the oven but do not remove the cheesecake for another hour. Remove to a wire rack and let cool to room temperature. Place the cheesecake on a large plate. Loosen from the side of the pan with a sharp knife and remove the side of the pan.

Yield: 8 servings
JANE BLUESTEIN

Holiday & Passover

GAMMY'S BLINTZ SOUFFLÉ

12 cheese blintzes	1/4 cup orange juice
6 eggs, beaten	2 teaspoons vanilla extract
2 cups sour cream	1 1/2 teaspoons salt
6 tablespoons sugar	

Arrange the blintzes in a lightly greased baking dish. Combine the eggs, sour cream, sugar, orange juice, vanilla and salt in a large mixing bowl and beat well. Pour evenly over the blintzes. Bake at 325 degrees for 1 hour or until golden brown and bubbly. Serve warm with a sauce of blueberry pie filling, water and lemon juice.

Yield: 8 to 10 servings

LYNNE AND MARK COHEN

Everyone knew it was Channukah when Papa (Nathan Epsman) would put a dish towel in his belt and begin to hand grate potatoes and onions early in the morning. As he began frying the potato latkes early in the evening, you could smell the wonderful aroma from the bottom of the driveway. Family and close friends would gather around where Papa was cooking—everyone laughing and talking. All the children would play in any available space in the kitchen. As quickly as Papa would take the latkes from the frying pan to drain, they would be eaten. He would laugh and continue to make them as long as we would eat them. At the same time, Gammy (Sylvia Epsman) would prepare her Blintz Soufflé, another family favorite. She never complained about too many people in the kitchen or too many cooks spoiling the broth. As we'd smell the Blintz Soufflé, we'd each open the oven. Every so often the Blintz Soufflé would fall before we ate it, but it was always delicious. Our family has so many fond memories of each holiday—lots of family and friends.

PAPA'S POTATO LATKES

5 pounds potatoes, peeled
6 eggs, beaten
4 onions, grated

1 cup matzo meal
1 teaspoon salt, or to taste
Vegetable oil for frying

Grate the potatoes into a large bowl; squeeze out excess water. Add the beaten eggs and grated onion and mix well. Stir in the matzo meal and salt. Heat 1/4 inch oil in a large (preferably black cast-iron) skillet. Drop the potato mixture by spoonfuls into the hot oil. Cook until golden brown and crispy on both sides. Remove with a spatula to paper towels to drain. Serve immediately with applesauce and sour cream.

Yield: (about) 4 dozen latkes
LYNNE AND MARK COHEN

POTATO LATKES

6 medium potatoes, peeled
1 small onion, grated (optional)
2 eggs, lightly beaten
1/4 cup (about) matzo meal
1 teaspoon salt

1/2 teaspoon baking powder
1/4 teaspoon pepper
Vegetable oil for frying
Applesauce or sour cream

Grate the potatoes into a large bowl; squeeze out excess water. Add the grated onion and eggs and mix well. Stir in the matzo meal, salt, baking powder and pepper. Heat oil in a large skillet. Drop the potato mixture by spoonfuls into the hot oil. Cook until golden brown on both sides. Remove with a spatula to paper towels to drain. Serve immediately with applesauce or sour cream.

Yield: (about) 3 dozen latkes
SHARON SAMEN

SWEET POTATO LATKES

2 pounds sweet potatoes or yams,
   peeled
2 tablespoons minced fresh gingerroot
4 green onions, finely chopped
2/3 cup all-purpose flour
1 1/2 teaspoons salt

1 teaspoon freshly ground black
   pepper
2 eggs, beaten
Vegetable oil for frying
Applesauce
Sour cream

Grate the potatoes coarsely into a large bowl; squeeze out excess water. Stir in the gingerroot and green onions. Mix the flour, salt and pepper in a bowl. Stir slowly into the potatoes. Add the eggs and mix well. Pour enough oil to generously cover the bottom of a large heavy skillet and place over medium-high heat until hot. Drop scant 1/4 cupfuls of the potato mixture into the hot oil. Flatten slightly with the back of a spatula to a 3-inch diameter latke. Cook until golden brown, about 4 minutes. Turn and cook for 3 to 4 minutes or until cooked through. Remove with a spatula to a baking sheet lined with 3 layers of paper towels. Keep warm in an oven at 225 degrees while cooking the remaining latkes. Serve with applesauce and sour cream.

Yield: 2 dozen latkes
SHERRON GOLDSTEIN

*Ted and Barbara,
Marissa and
Harold Apolinsky,
Sherron and
Allan Goldstein*

POTATO AND APPLE LATKES WITH SMOKED SALMON AND FRESH THYME

1 pound russet potatoes (about 5 medium), peeled
1 medium onion
1 Granny Smith apple, peeled
1 egg, beaten
1 green onion, finely chopped
1 tablespoon chopped fresh thyme

Salt and pepper to taste
1/4 cup all-purpose flour
Vegetable oil for frying
1 cup sour cream
2 tablespoons prepared horseradish
8 ounces thinly sliced smoked salmon
Chopped fresh chives to taste

Grate the potatoes, onion and apple coarsely in a food processor. Remove to a colander lined with a kitchen towel. Wrap the towel around the mixture and squeeze to remove as much liquid as possible. Mix the drained potato mixture, egg, green onion and thyme in a large bowl. Season with salt and pepper. Add the flour and toss to mix. Pour enough oil to generously cover the bottom of a large heavy skillet and place over medium-high heat until hot. Drop scant 1/4 cupfuls of the potato mixture into the hot oil. Flatten slightly with the back of a spatula to a 3-inch diameter latke. Cook until golden brown, about 4 minutes. Turn and cook for 3 to 4 minutes or until cooked through. Remove with a spatula to a baking sheet lined with 3 layers of paper towels. Keep warm in an oven at 225 degrees while cooking the remaining latkes. Discard any liquid remaining in the bowl. Mix the sour cream and horseradish in a small bowl. Arrange 2 to 3 latkes on a plate. Top with a dollop of horseradish cream, a slice of smoked salmon and a sprinkle of chopped chives. Serve immediately.

Yield: 6 to 8 servings
SHERRON GOLDSTEIN

Koplon and Barstein Family

157

LORAINE'S DOUBLE-APPLE NOODLE KUGEL

16 ounces egg noodles	3/4 cup sugar
1/4 cup (1/2 stick) butter or margarine, melted	1 teaspoon vanilla extract
	1 1/2 teaspoons cinnamon
1 cup applesauce (no sugar added)	1/2 cup raisins
4 eggs	4 Granny Smith apples, peeled,
2 egg whites	cored, quartered, thinly sliced

Cook the noodles according to package directions except cook for several minutes less than stated. Drain and return to the saucepan. Add the butter and applesauce and toss to coat. Whisk the eggs, egg whites, sugar, vanilla and cinnamon in a large bowl. Stir in the noodles, raisins and apples. Spread into a 9x13-inch baking dish coated with nonstick cooking spray. Cover with a sheet of foil coated with nonstick cooking spray. Chill overnight, if desired. Bake, covered, at 350 degrees for 45 minutes. Remove the foil and spray the top of the kugel with nonstick cooking spray. Increase the oven temperature to 375 degrees and bake for 20 minutes or until lightly browned. Remove to a wire rack and let cool for 15 minutes before cutting. Serve warm or at room temperature.

Yield: 12 servings
LORAINE REZNIK

APRICOT NOODLE KUGEL

6 eggs
8 ounces cream cheese, softened
1/2 cup (1 stick) butter or margarine,
　softened
2 cups sour cream
1 cup sugar
16 ounces wide noodles, cooked,
　drained

1 (16-ounce) can whole apricots,
　drained, pitted, chopped
1 (16-ounce) can apricot halves,
　drained, some liquid reserved
Sugar to taste
Cinnamon to taste
Crushed graham cracker crumbs
　to taste

Place the eggs in a blender and blend until well beaten. Add the cream cheese, butter, sour cream and 1 cup sugar. Blend until well mixed. Pour into a large bowl. Stir in the noodles and chopped apricots. Spoon into a greased 3-quart baking dish. Arrange the apricot halves on top. Sprinkle with sugar to taste, cinnamon, graham cracker crumbs and a little of the reserved apricot liquid. Bake at 350 degrees for 1 hour.

Yield: 12 servings
GLADYS EPSTEIN

NOODLE KUGEL

16 ounces wide noodles
Salt to taste
3 quarts water
1 cup (2 sticks) butter, melted
9 jumbo eggs
24 ounces large curd cottage cheese
1 1/2 cups sugar

1/2 teaspoon salt
2 cups sugar frosted cornflake cereal,
　crushed
2 tablespoons cinnamon-sugar
1/2 cup (1 stick) butter, cut into
　pieces

Add the noodles to a large pot of boiling salted water. Return to a boil and cook for 3 minutes. Remove from the heat and cover. Let stand for 9 minutes. Drain well and toss in a bowl with 1 cup melted butter. Stir the eggs, cottage cheese, sugar and 1/2 teaspoon salt in a large bowl. Fold in the noodles. Spoon into a buttered 9×13-inch baking dish. Cover with the cereal and sprinkle with the cinnamon-sugar. Top with 1/2 cup butter pieces. Bake at 350 degrees for 1 hour.

Yield: 12 servings
SHARON SAMEN

NOODLE KUGEL

12 ounces wide egg noodles, cooked, drained

1/4 cup (1/2 stick) butter, melted

8 ounces cream cheese, softened

1 cup sour cream

1 cup sugar

4 eggs

1 (20-ounce) can juice-pack crushed pineapple, drained

3 cups sugar frosted cornflake cereal, coarsely crushed

1/4 cup (1/2 stick) butter, melted

1 tablespoon cinnamon

Toss the noodles with 1/4 cup melted butter in a bowl. Spread in a 9×13-inch baking dish. Combine the cream cheese, sour cream, sugar and eggs in a food processor. Process until smooth. Stir in the drained pineapple. Pour over the noodles and gently mix. Stir the cereal, 1/4 cup melted butter and cinnamon in a bowl. Spread on top of the noodle mixture. Bake at 350 degrees for 50 to 60 minutes or just until firm.

Yield: 12 servings

SHERRON GOLDSTEIN

POTATO KUGEL

2 pounds peeled potatoes (weigh after peeling)

1 onion

4 eggs

3 tablespoons matzo meal

3 tablespoons butter, melted

1 teaspoon baking powder

3/4 teaspoon salt

1/4 teaspoon pepper

Grate the potatoes and onion in a food processor fitted with the grating blade. Remove to a bowl. Finely chop the grated potato and onion in batches in a food processor fitted with the steel blade. Squeeze to remove excess liquid. Combine the potato mixture, eggs, matzo meal, melted butter, baking powder, salt and pepper in a bowl. Stir to mix well. Spoon into greased muffin tins. Bake at 350 degrees for 45 minutes. Increase the oven temperature to 375 degrees and bake for 15 minutes or until golden brown.

Yield: 12 potato kugels

JANN BLITZ

POTATO KUGEL

6 large potatoes, peeled, grated
1 large onion, grated
2 eggs
1/2 cup all-purpose flour

1 1/2 teaspoons salt
1/2 teaspoon baking powder
1/4 cup vegetable oil

Squeeze the grated potatoes and onions to remove excess liquid. Combine the potatoes, onions and eggs in a bowl. Stir until well mixed. Sift the flour, salt and baking powder into the bowl and mix well. Stir in the oil. Spoon into a lightly greased baking dish. Bake at 350 degrees for 1 hour or until crisp and golden brown.

Yield: 6 servings
LYNNE AND MARK COHEN

For as long as I can remember until 1973, we would go to Bebe and Papa Epsman's southside home for Sunday lunch and spend the day. It was always the same menu, but we all looked forward to it and loved being there. Bebe Epsman's kugel was delicious!

Justin, Mark, Lynne, Cecily and Jonathan Cohen

HOLIDAY BRISKET OF BEEF

1 envelope onion soup mix
1 1/2 cups water
1/2 cup ketchup
2 large onions, sliced
1 whole garlic bulb, peeled, minced
12 sprigs fresh thyme
2 tablespoons salt-free all-purpose
    seasoning
2 tablespoons Beau Monde
    seasoning
Salt and freshly cracked pepper
    to taste

1 (5- to 6-pound) beef brisket,
    fat trimmed
6 carrots, peeled, sliced
4 parsnips, peeled, sliced
4 ribs celery, sliced
1 bulb fennel, quartered
3/4 cup chopped fresh parsley
3 cups red wine or low-sodium
    beef broth
Additional carrots, celery and
    peeled potatoes

Mix the onion soup mix, water and ketchup in a bowl. Pour into a roasting pan. Top with the onion slices and garlic. Arrange the sprigs of thyme over the onions. Mix the all-purpose seasoning and Beau Monde seasoning in a small bowl. Season with salt and cracked pepper. Rub this mixture all over the beef. Place the beef in the roasting pan. Add the carrots, parsnips, celery, fennel, parsley and wine to the pan and cover. Bake at 325 degrees for 2 1/2 hours or until almost done. Remove the meat to a cutting board and let stand for a few minutes. Strain the pan juices and discard the vegetables. Remove the fat from the gravy, if possible. Slice the beef and return to the roasting pan. Add the strained gravy, additional carrots, celery and potatoes and cover. Bake at 325 degrees for 40 to 60 minutes or until the beef is tender.

Note: This recipe can be made 1 day ahead, up to the final roasting. Chill, covered, until ready to cook.

Yield: 10 to 12 servings
SHERRON GOLDSTEIN

COMPANY BRISKET

2 tablespoons sugar or artificial
  sweetener
1 (7- to 10-pound) beef brisket
2 tablespoons all-purpose flour
1 (1-ounce) envelope onion
  soup mix
4 bay leaves

Garlic to taste
Freshly ground pepper to taste
2 (16-ounce) cans jellied cranberry
  sauce
Chopped peeled potatoes to taste
Chopped carrots to taste

Sprinkle the sugar over the beef. Add the flour to a large oven-cooking bag and shake to distribute the flour. Place the beef in the bag, fat side up. Sprinkle the soup mix over the beef. Add the bay leaves. Season generously with garlic and pepper. Spread the cranberry sauce over the beef. Fill one empty cranberry sauce can with water and add the water to the bag. Seal the bag and cut several small slits in the top of the bag. Place in a large baking pan. Bake at 325 to 350 degrees for 45 minutes to 1 hour per pound. Remove from the oven about 1 hour before the roast is done. Open the bag carefully and add the potatoes and carrots. Reseal the bag and return to the oven for about 1 hour or until the beef is tender and the vegetables are cooked. Slice and serve with the gravy from the bag.

Note: This roast can be made the day before and reheated. Also freezes well.

Yield: 16 to 20 servings
ELLEN DORSKY

Ellen and Jack Dorsky celebrating an anniversary dinner at the home of Ellen's mother and dad, Bessie and Arnold Siegal. Our family celebrated every Jewish holiday, birthday, and anniversary.

163

BEST BRISKET

1 (3-pound) beef brisket
1 (1-ounce) envelope onion
   soup mix

1 (16-ounce) can jellied cranberry
   sauce
Pepper to taste

Place the beef in a roasting pan. Sprinkle with the onion soup mix. Spread the cranberry sauce over the beef. Fill the empty cranberry sauce can halfway with water and pour into the bottom of the roasting pan around the beef. Season with pepper. Cover tightly with foil. Bake at 350 degrees for 3 hours. Remove the beef to a cutting board and let cool. Slice the beef and put back into the juices. Chill, covered, overnight. Reheat when ready to serve.

Yield: 6 to 8 servings
MACKIE HOROWITZ

SWEET-AND-SOUR BRISKET

2 cups boiling water
1/2 cup sugar
Juice of 2 or 3 lemons
1 tablespoon dill seed
2 bay leaves

Salt and pepper to taste
Sour salt to taste
1 onion, thinly sliced
1 (3-pound) beef brisket

Combine the boiling water, sugar, lemon juice, dill seed and bay leaves in a roasting pan. Season with salt, pepper and sour salt. Add the onion slices and beef. Cook over medium heat for 45 minutes, turning the meat often. Add more water, if needed. Remove from the stovetop and bake at 350 degrees for 2 1/2 to 3 hours. Baste often and add more lemon juice, sugar or sour salt if desired.

Yield: 6 to 8 servings
JUDY ABROMS

My mother-in-law, Ruth Abroms, was born in Perry, the territory of Oklahoma before it became a state. She moved to Louisville and as an adult and wife to Dermott, Arkansas. Her mother, Freida, moved in with her and did most of the cooking. This old world recipe traveled from Bialystok to Dermott and finally home to Birmingham, AL. We all loved it! Hope you do, too.

Meat Filling I
Leftover cooked meat, ground
Ginger to taste
Prepared mustard to taste
Salt and pepper to taste
Broth or water

Meat Filling II
Chopped onions to taste
Ground beef to taste
Salt and pepper to taste

Dough
$1/2$ cup vegetable oil
1 egg
$3/4$ teaspoon salt
$1/2$ to $2/3$ cup cold water
$2^1/2$ cups all-purpose flour
$3^1/2$ teaspoons baking powder

For meat filling I, place the meat in a bowl. Season with ginger, prepared mustard, salt and pepper. Stir to mix. Add a small amount of broth if mixture seems too dry.

For meat filling II, sauté the onions and ground beef in a skillet until the onions are tender and the meat is cooked through. Season with salt and pepper.

For the dough, beat the oil and egg in a bowl until well mixed. Beat in the salt and cold water. Sift the flour and baking powder into a bowl. Beat into the egg mixture to form a dough. Roll out the dough on a lightly floured surface. Cut into squares. Place about 1 teaspoon of meat filling in the center of the squares and fold over. Seal the edges and prick with a fork. Place on a greased baking sheet. Bake at 400 degrees until golden brown. Serve with soup.

Yield: (about) 2 dozen perogen
SANDRA L. VINIK

MEAT BLINTZES

2 cups water
4 eggs
1 teaspoon salt
1 cup sifted all-purpose flour
1/4 teaspoon baking powder

Vegetable oil
Finely chopped cooked beef brisket
    or pot roast
Finely chopped onion
Salt and pepper to taste

Combine the water, eggs, 1 teaspoon salt, flour and baking powder in a blender and process until smooth. Heat 2 tablespoons oil in a small skillet. Add enough batter to cover the bottom of the skillet. Cook until the bottom is lightly browned and the blintz is cooked through. Turn out onto a work surface and let cool. Repeat until all the batter is used, adding more oil to the skillet as needed. Sauté the beef and onion in a skillet until browned. Season with salt to taste and pepper. Spoon some of the meat mixture onto one end of each blintz. Fold in the sides and roll up.

Yield: (about) 2 dozen blintzes
BARBARA BETTEN

Jerry and Jean
Sklar with
Suzanne, Brad
and Stephanie

TZIMMES (RABBI MILLER'S FAVORITE)

4 pounds beef short ribs
Vegetable oil
2 (32-ounce) bags baby carrots
4 sweet potatoes, peeled, quartered

1 onion, quartered
3/4 cup sugar, or to taste
2 to 3 (12-ounce) boxes pitted
   prunes

Brown the short ribs in a small amount of oil in a large saucepan. Add the carrots, sweet potatoes, onion, sugar and prunes. Add water to cover halfway. Reduce the heat to low and cook for 3 to 5 hours or until the meat is tender. Add more water if necessary during cooking. Remove from the heat and let cool. Chill, covered, until the fat solidifies on the surface. Remove the fat and discard. Cook over medium heat until hot.

Yield: 16 to 20 servings
JUDI SCHULMAN-MILLER

*Susan, Kelly and
Karl Biedinger*

CHICKEN SOUP WITH MATZO BALLS

Chicken Soup

2 (3-pound) chickens, cut up, skin
    and fat removed
Salt and freshly ground pepper
    to taste
2 large onions, quartered
6 carrots, peeled, sliced
1 large parsnip, peeled, cut into
    1-inch pieces
5 large ribs celery, including leaves,
    halved
2 garlic cloves, halved
1 bay leaf
1/2 bunch fresh parsley, tied with
    white thread

Matzo Balls

1/4 cup vegetable oil
4 eggs, lightly beaten
1 chicken bouillon cube, crushed
1/4 cup dried parsley flakes
Salt and pepper to taste
1 cup matzo meal
2 tablespoons chicken soup
2 tablespoons lemon-lime soda
    or club soda

For the soup, place the chicken pieces in a large stockpot. Add water to cover
the chicken by 2 inches. Season with salt and pepper. Bring to a boil. Skim off
the foam. Add the onions, carrots, parsnip, celery, garlic and bay leaf. Reduce the
heat and cover. Cook for 1 1/2 hours or until the chicken is tender, skimming the
foam during cooking. Add the parsley and cook for 15 minutes. Season with salt
and pepper. Pour the soup through a sieve into a large saucepan. Add only the
cooked carrots to the broth. Discard remaining vegetables. Reserve the cooked
chicken for another use. Chill, covered, until the fat solidifies on the surface.
Remove the fat and discard. Cook over medium heat until hot.

    For the matzo balls, beat the oil and eggs in a bowl. Stir in the crushed
bouillon cube and parsley. Season with salt and pepper. Stir in the matzo meal
gradually. Add the soup and soda and mix well. Chill, covered, for 1 hour. Dip
hands in a bowl of water and then make 2-inch diameter matzo balls. Bring a
4-quart saucepan of water to a simmer. Add the matzo balls and cover the pot.
Simmer for 30 minutes, do not uncover. Remove to a colander to drain and
add to the chicken soup.

Yield: 6 servings

SHERRON GOLDSTEIN

168

YOM TOV CHICKEN SOUP (JEWISH PENICILLIN)

3 chicken breasts
5 potatoes, peeled
5 carrots
1 tablespoon chopped fresh parsley
1 tablespoon chopped celery leaves

1 cup white wine
Onion salt to taste
Celery salt to taste
Pepper to taste

Place the chicken, potatoes, carrots, parsley and celery leaves in a large saucepan. Add water to cover. Bring to a boil. Reduce the heat and simmer until the chicken is cooked through and the vegetables are soft. Remove the chicken and vegetables to a large platter to cool. Chill the broth, covered, until the fat solidifies on the surface. Remove the fat and discard. Remove the chicken from the bones, discarding the bones and skin. Purée the cooked chicken, potatoes and carrots in a food processor or blender. Add to the soup. Heat over medium heat until hot. Stir in the wine. Season with onion salt, celery salt and pepper.

Yield: 6 servings
SANDRA VINIK

Sherron and Allan Goldstein family

CHOPPED LIVER

1 to 2 tablespoons shmaltz,
 vegetable oil or butter
2 large onions, chopped
 (about 1 pound)
1 to 2 tablespoons shmaltz,
 vegetable oil or butter
1 pound chicken livers

4 hard-cooked eggs
 (2 yolks discarded), chopped
Salt and pepper to taste
1/4 cup chopped fresh parsley
Parsley sprigs
Crackers or cocktail rye bread

Melt 1 to 2 tablespoons shmaltz in a heavy skillet. Add the onions and sauté over medium heat until soft and light golden brown. Remove to a bowl. Add 1 to 2 tablespoons shmaltz to the skillet. Add the chicken livers and sauté until no trace of pink remains. Process the chicken livers, onions and hard-cooked eggs in batches in a food processor, pulsing a few times just until coarsely chopped. Remove to a bowl. Season with salt and pepper. Stir in the chopped parsley. Add additional shmaltz or oil if the spread seems too dry. Spoon the chopped liver into a serving bowl and garnish with parsley sprigs. Serve with crackers.

Yield: (about) 3 cups
SHERRON GOLDSTEIN

Rosh Hashanah Turkey

1 large turkey
Pepper to taste
1 (1-ounce) envelope brown gravy
　　mix
French mustard (enough to coat
　　the turkey)

1 (12-ounce) jar apricot preserves
1 (1-ounce) envelope brown gravy
　　mix or cornstarch
1/2 cup lemon juice

Place the turkey on a rack in a roasting pan. Season with pepper. Stir 1 envelope brown gravy mix, French mustard and half the apricot preserves in a bowl. Spread over the turkey to coat. Roast at 325 degrees until cooked through, basting occasionally. Remove the turkey to a platter. Coat with the remaining apricot preserves and chill until ready to serve. Remove the drippings to a small saucepan. Chill until the fat solidifies on the surface. Remove the fat and discard. Add water to the drippings to ensure enough gravy and heat over medium heat. Stir in 1 envelope of brown gravy mix to thicken the gravy. Stir in the lemon juice. Reheat the turkey in a shallow pan at 300 degrees. Place under the broiler for a few minutes to brown.

Yield: variable
SANDRA VINIK

MOMMA RUTH'S MANDEL BREAD

4 eggs
1 cup vegetable oil
1 1/3 cups sugar
2 teaspoons (or more) vanilla extract
1 teaspoon (or more) almond extract

4 cups all-purpose flour
1 1/2 teaspoons baking powder
1/2 teaspoon salt
2 cups (or more) chopped pecans
2 teaspoons vegetable oil

Beat the eggs in a large bowl with an electric mixer at high speed until pale yellow. Add 1 cup oil and the sugar while beating. Beat in the vanilla and almond extract at low speed. Sift the flour, baking powder and salt into a bowl. Beat in the dry ingredients and pecans. Chill the dough, covered, overnight. Coat 2 baking sheets with nonstick cooking spray. Add 1 teaspoon oil to each sheet and spread to coat. Divide the dough into 6 balls. Roll each ball on a work surface to a log shape. Arrange 3 logs on each baking sheet. Bake at 350 degrees for 15 to 20 minutes or until lightly browned and firm. Remove to a work surface and slice the logs. Arrange the slices on the baking sheets, cut side down. Bake at 250 degrees for 35 to 45 minutes. Remove rounds to a wire rack to cool. Store in an airtight container when cool.

Yield: 36 servings
JUDY ROTENSTREICH

Judy Rotenstreich,
Rose Rotenstreich,
Roslyn Toranto Levene

172

MANDEL BREAD

3 eggs
1 cup sugar
1 cup vegetable oil
1 teaspoon vanilla extract
1 teaspoon almond extract

3 cups sifted all-purpose flour
1 teaspoon baking powder
1 cup chopped almonds
Cinnamon-sugar to taste

Beat the eggs lightly in a large bowl. Stir in the sugar. Add the oil and mix. Stir in the vanilla and almond extract. Mix the flour, baking powder and almonds in a bowl. Stir into the egg mixture gradually and mix to a sticky dough. Chill, covered, until firm. Divide the dough into 6 sections. Roll each section on floured waxed paper into a long loaf. Arrange the loaves on a baking sheet coated with oil. Bake at 325 degrees for 30 to 40 minutes. Remove loaves to a work surface and cut into slices. Sprinkle each side of the slices with cinnamon-sugar. Arrange the slices on the baking sheets, cut side down. Bake at 325 degrees for 5 to 7 minutes. Turn the slices over and bake for 5 to 7 minutes longer. Remove slices to a wire rack to cool.

Yield: (about) 28 slices
IRMA K. KOCH

MANDEL BREAD

1 cup shortening
1 cup vegetable oil
2 cups sugar
6 eggs
1 1/2 teaspoons vanilla extract
1 1/2 teaspoons lemon juice

5 to 6 cups all-purpose flour
2 (heaping) teaspoons baking
   powder
Pinch of salt
1 cup chopped walnuts or pecans

Beat the shortening, oil and sugar in a large bowl. Beat in the eggs, vanilla and lemon juice. Mix the flour, baking powder and salt in a bowl. Stir into the egg mixture. Add the walnuts and mix well. Chill for 1 hour. Shape the dough with oiled hands into long narrow rolls and place on a greased baking sheet. Bake at 350 degrees for 20 to 25 minutes. Remove the rolls to a work surface and cut into 1/2-inch slices. Arrange on the baking sheet, cut side down. Bake at 325 degrees for 15 minutes. Remove slices to a wire rack to cool.

Yield: (about) 4 dozen slices
SARAH HALPERN

Our Mother, Grace Macknin, was an adorable person, a marvelous businesswoman, and so much fun. She was also a very loving mother; therefore, when we found this recipe (circa 1945) among her papers, in her own handwriting, it became very precious to us. She knew how to make the Mandel Breit so only felt the need to write down the ingredients.
—Mama Grace's daughters, Roz Caplan and
Bernice Perlman

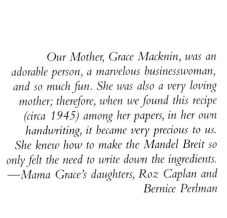

CHAROSES

4 to 5 large red or green apples,
   peeled, cored
1/2 cup pecans or walnuts, chopped

3 to 4 tablespoons sugar
1/2 to 1 teaspoon cinnamon
5 tablespoons sweet red wine

Grate the apples into a bowl. Add the pecans, sugar, cinnamon and wine. Mix well.
   Note: If using a food processor to grate the apples and chop the nuts, be careful not to overprocess.

Yield: (about) 5 cups
JULIE MARKS

ALANA'S FAVORITE GELATIN MOLD

2 (3-ounce) packages raspberry
   gelatin
2 cups water
2 (16-ounce) cans whole
   cranberry sauce

1 (11-ounce) can mandarin oranges,
   drained

Dissolve the gelatin in the water in a bowl. Stir in the cranberry sauce and oranges. Pour into a 2-quart mold and chill until firm.

Yield: 8 servings
JUDI SCHULMAN-MILLER

APPLE MATZO KUGEL

5 sheets matzo
3 egg yolks
1/2 cup sugar
1/2 teaspoon cinnamon
1/4 teaspoon salt
3 egg whites
1/4 cup raisins (optional)

3 tablespoons margarine
4 tart apples, peeled, cored,
    thinly sliced
Cinnamon-sugar to taste
1/4 cup chopped nuts
Margarine to taste

Soak the matzo in water; drain well. Beat the egg yolks in a bowl until pale yellow. Beat in the sugar, cinnamon and salt. Stir in the drained matzo. Beat the egg whites in a bowl until stiff. Fold into the egg yolk mixture along with the raisins. Melt 3 tablespoons margarine in a rectangular baking dish in the oven. Tilt the dish to coat the bottom. Spread 3/4 of the batter in the hot baking dish. Top with the apples. Sprinkle with cinnamon-sugar and half the nuts. Top with the remaining batter and dot with margarine to taste. Sprinkle with additional cinnamon-sugar and the remaining nuts. Bake at 350 degrees for about 45 minutes. Remove to a wire rack to cool.

Yield: 8 servings
JULIE MARKS

HONEY CAKE

4 cups sifted all-purpose flour
1 tablespoon baking cocoa
2 teaspoons baking powder
1 1/2 teaspoons baking soda
1/2 teaspoon ground cloves
1/2 teaspoon allspice
1/2 teaspoon ginger
1/2 teaspoon cinnamon

1/2 cup walnuts or pecans, chopped
1/2 cup golden raisins
1 1/2 cups sugar
5 eggs, or equivalent amount of
  egg substitute
1/2 cup vegetable oil
1 (16-ounce) jar dark honey
1 cup strong brewed coffee

Whisk the flour, baking cocoa, baking powder, baking soda, cloves, allspice, ginger and cinnamon in a bowl. Stir in the walnuts and raisins. Beat the sugar and eggs in large bowl with an electric mixer until light and fluffy. Beat in the oil gradually. Mix the honey and coffee in a bowl. Add to the egg mixture and beat until blended. Add the dry ingredients gradually and beat until well mixed. Spoon into a greased 9×13-inch cake pan or bundt pan. Bake at 350 degrees for 1 hour or until a wooden pick inserted in the center comes out clean. Remove to a wire rack to cool.

Yield: 12 servings
SHERRON GOLDSTEIN

KICHLACH

6 eggs	Pinch of salt
1 tablespoon vegetable oil	3 1/2 to 3 3/4 cups all-purpose flour
2 teaspoons sugar	Sugar

Whisk the eggs, oil, 2 teaspoons sugar and salt in a bowl. Stir in the flour to make a soft dough. Sprinkle a work surface with sugar. Roll out the dough very thinly over the sugar. Cut into diamond shapes. Heat a cookie sheet at 500 degrees. Remove from the oven and sprinkle with sugar. Place the cutout shapes over the hot sugar. Sprinkle tops with sugar. Bake at 500 degrees for 10 minutes or until golden brown, watching carefully to prevent burning. Remove kichlach to a wire rack to cool.

Yield: (about) 5 dozen
SANDRA VINIK

RUGALEH

8 ounces cream cheese, softened	1 (12-ounce) jar apricot jam
1 cup (2 sticks) butter, softened	1 cup pecans, finely chopped
2 cups all-purpose flour	1 cup golden raisins
2 tablespoons sugar	1 cup sugar
1/2 cup (1 stick) butter or margarine, melted	2 tablespoons cinnamon
	Confectioners' sugar

Mix the cream cheese, 1 cup butter, flour and 2 tablespoons sugar in a bowl until well blended. Divide the dough into 4 sections. Dust with flour and roll into 4 balls. Cover with waxed paper and chill for 1 hour. Roll out each ball between sheets of waxed paper to a 10×15-inch rectangle. Brush with some of the melted butter. Spread the jam over the rectangles, leaving a 1-inch plain border around the edges. Mix the pecans, raisins, 1 cup sugar and cinnamon in a bowl. Sprinkle over the jam. Roll up as for jelly rolls and place on a baking sheet, seam side down. Brush with the remaining melted butter. Bake at 375 degrees for 20 minutes or until the tops are golden brown. Remove the rolls to a wire rack to cool. Slice when cool and dust with confectioners' sugar.

Yield: (about) 4 dozen
SHERRON GOLDSTEIN

CHALLAH

1 envelope dry yeast
$1/4$ cup warm water
$1/2$ cup sugar
1 teaspoon salt
$1/4$ cup vegetable oil
1 cup hot water

2 eggs
5 cups unsifted bread flour
1 egg yolk
1 tablespoon water
Poppy seeds

Dissolve the yeast in $1/4$ cup warm water in a small bowl. Combine the sugar, salt and oil in a large bowl and mix well. Add 1 cup hot water and stir until the sugar is dissolved. Cool to warm.

Add the eggs and yeast mixture and mix well. Add $4^{1}/2$ cups of the bread flour and mix to form a dough, adding the remaining $1/2$ cup bread flour if needed to clean the bowl. Cover with waxed paper or a damp cloth. Let rise for 2 to $2^{1}/2$ hours or until doubled in bulk. Punch the dough down. Divide into 4 equal portions. Roll each portion between your hands to form a strand 21 inches long. Arrange the 4 strands lengthwise on a greased baking sheet, pinching the tops of the strands together. Bring the strand on the right over the next strand, under the third strand and over the fourth strand. Repeat always starting with the strand on the right until the braid is complete. Trim the ends evenly and tuck underneath. Cover with waxed paper. Spray with nonstick cooking spray. Let rise for 2 hours or until doubled in bulk.

Beat the egg yolk and 1 tablespoon water in a bowl. Brush over the braided loaf using a pastry brush. Sprinkle with poppy seeds.

Bake at 350 degrees for 30 to 35 minutes or until a wooden pick inserted into the center comes out clean.

Note: You may also make 1 round Challah by punching down the dough and making 1 long strand about 2 inches in diameter. Coil the strand like a snake and continue baking as above.

Yield: 1 braided loaf
LORI DORSKY

This recipe was handed down to me by my Aunt Razelle Toranto. We always looked forward to Friday night dinners and homemade Challah. Our tradition is to say the Hamotzi and then tear off a piece of Challah and pass that piece around to share with everyone at the table. Aunt Razelle's sister, Marion, taught her the recipe. She makes Challahs professionally and they are truly works of art as well as delicious to eat.

BLINTZ DELIGHT

2 (13-ounce) packages frozen cheese
   blintzes, thawed (12 blintzes)
1/2 cup (1 stick) margarine, melted
1 cup egg substitute

1 1/2 cups light sour cream
1 teaspoon vanilla extract
1/4 cup sugar

Arrange the blintzes, seam side down, in a single layer in a 2-quart baking dish.
Stir the melted margarine, egg substitute, sour cream, vanilla and sugar in a bowl.
Pour over the blintzes. Bake at 350 degrees for 45 minutes.

Yield: 6 servings
HANNAH GOLDSTEIN

*Standing left to right:
Sidney Goldstein,
Morris Goldstein,
Hyman Goldstein,
Arthur Goldstein,
Julius Goldstein.
Seated left to right:
Myra Goldstein,
Bessie Goldstein,
Hannah Goldstein,
Nancy Goldstein,
Muriel Goldstein.*

MAMA LENORA'S BLINTZ SOUFFLÉ

1/2 cup (1 stick) unsalted butter or
    margarine
12 eggs
3 cups light (not fat-free) sour cream
2 teaspoons pure vanilla extract
1 (scant) cup sugar

2 teaspoons salt
2/3 cup orange juice
2 (13-ounce) packages frozen cheese
    blintzes (12 blintzes)
Cinnamon-sugar

Melt the butter in a 9x13-inch baking dish or pan in the oven. Pour the melted butter into a large bowl, leaving enough to coat the bottom and sides of the baking dish. Add the eggs, sour cream, vanilla, sugar, salt and orange juice to the bowl. Beat with an electric mixer for 3 to 5 minutes or until creamy. Arrange the frozen blintzes in the bottom of the heated baking dish. Pour the egg mixture over the blintzes and sprinkle with cinnamon-sugar. Bake at 350 degrees for 65 to 75 minutes. Do not open the oven during baking. Serve immediately.

Yield: 6 servings
NATALIE HAUSMAN-WEISS

BUBBE'S BLINTZES

5 eggs	1 egg
1¹/2 cups water	8 ounces cream cheese, softened
1 teaspoon sugar	15 ounces farmer cheese
¹/2 teaspoon salt	1 teaspoon sugar
1¹/2 cups all-purpose flour	1 teaspoon vanilla extract
Vegetable oil	

Beat 5 eggs, water, 1 teaspoon sugar and salt in a bowl. Stir in the flour. Heat a small amount of oil in a 6-inch skillet. Add enough batter to cover the bottom of the skillet. Cook until the crepe is cooked through. Turn out onto a work surface and let cool. Repeat until all the batter is used, adding more oil to the skillet as needed. Mix 1 egg, cream cheese, farmer cheese and 1 teaspoon sugar in a bowl. Stir in the vanilla. Spread 1 tablespoon of the filling on each crepe. Turn in the sides and roll up. Arrange the blintzes in a baking dish. Bake at 425 degrees until golden brown.

Yield: (about) 2 dozen blintzes

LOUISE NAGRODZKI ABROMS

MINI BLINTZES

*3 loaves sliced white bread, crusts
trimmed*
16 ounces cream cheese, softened
2 egg yolks
1/2 cup sugar

*1 cup (2 sticks) butter or margarine,
melted*
Cinnamon-sugar
1 cup sour cream

Roll each slice of bread with a rolling pin on a work surface until very thin. Mix the cream cheese, egg yolks and sugar in a bowl. Spread over the thin bread slices. Roll up as for a jelly roll and cut in half. Dip into the melted butter and then cinnamon-sugar. Arrange in a greased baking dish. Bake at 350 degrees for 10 to 15 minutes or until lightly browned. Serve with the sour cream for dipping.

Note: Can be frozen before baking.

Yield: (about) 8 dozen mini blintzes
KIM ROSEMORE

HAMANTASHEN

2 cups sugar
1 cup vegetable oil
4 eggs
1/4 cup orange juice
6 cups all-purpose flour
2 heaping teaspoons baking powder
Pinch of salt
Mixed dried fruits, such as prunes,
    raisins, apricots and nuts, ground

1 1/2 cups sugar
2 tablespoons honey
Grated zest of 1 lemon
Apricot preserves to taste
Orange marmalade to taste
1 egg white

Mix 2 cups sugar and oil in a large bowl. Stir in the eggs and orange juice and mix well. Sift the flour, baking powder and salt into a bowl. Stir into the egg mixture to form a dough. Divide the dough into 4 sections. Roll out each section on a floured work surface to 1/8 inch thick. Cut into 2 1/2-inch circles. Mix the ground fruit and nuts, 1 1/2 cups sugar, honey, lemon zest, apricot preserves and orange marmalade in a bowl. Place 1 heaping teaspoon of the fruit filling in the center of each circle. Lift and pinch the dough at 3 points on the circle to make a triangle to hold the filling. Beat the egg white with a small amount of water in a bowl. Brush onto the cookies. Place on a greased cookie sheet. Bake at 350 degrees for 15 to 20 minutes. Remove the cookies to a wire rack to cool.

Yield: 5 to 6 dozen cookies
SARAH HALPERN

HAMENTASHEN

3½ cups all-purpose flour
1 tablespoon baking powder
¼ teaspoon salt
½ cup (1 stick) butter, softened
1 cup sugar
2 eggs
¼ cup orange juice
1 (12-ounce) box pitted prunes,
    chopped

1 (11-ounce) package dried apricots,
    chopped
½ cup raisins
1 tablespoon lemon juice
3 tablespoons sugar
¼ teaspoon cinnamon

Mix the flour, baking powder and salt in a bowl. Beat the butter and 1 cup sugar in a large bowl. Add the eggs 1 at a time, beating well after each addition. Stir in the dry ingredients alternately with the orange juice, beginning and ending with the dry ingredients. Divide the dough in half and wrap in waxed paper. Chill for a few hours or until firm. Roll out the dough thinly on a floured surface. Cut into 4-inch rounds. Mix the prunes, apricots, raisins, lemon juice, 3 tablespoons sugar and cinnamon in a bowl. Place 1 heaping teaspoon of the fruit filling in the center of each circle. Lift and pinch the dough at 3 points on the circle to make a triangle to hold the filling. Place on a parchment-lined cookie sheet. Bake at 350 degrees for 15 minutes. Remove the cookies to a wire rack to cool. Store in a non-airtight container.

Note: There should be enough fruit filling left over to fill another batch of cookies.

Yield: (about) 4 dozen cookies
ANN MOLENGARTEN

This is the original recipe used by the Temple Youth Group when they used to sell hamentashen as a fund-raiser. The recipe came from one of the devoted sisterhood moms (don't know who), that used to help a bunch of inexperienced teen-aged cooks whip up hundreds of these each Purim to sell.

PASSOVER FRUIT COMPOTE

2 (16-ounce) cans lite peach slices
2 (16-ounce) cans lite pear halves
1 (17-ounce) can lite apricot halves
1 (15¼-ounce) can pineapple
   chunks
1 (16-ounce) can pitted dark
   cherries
3 to 4 bananas

Lemon juice to taste
2 cups pecan pieces
1 (10-ounce) can macaroons
¼ cup (½ stick) butter
½ cup packed brown sugar
⅓ to ½ cup banana liqueur or
   peach schnapps

Drain the peaches, pears, apricots, pineapple and cherries in a large colander.
Let stand over a bowl overnight in the refrigerator to drain well. Remove the
drained fruit to a large bowl. Slice the bananas and sprinkle with lemon juice in
a bowl. Toss gently to coat the bananas. Add the bananas and pecans to the fruit.
Toss gently to mix. Spoon half the fruit mixture into a 4-quart baking dish.
Crumble half the macaroons over the top. Cut the butter into the brown sugar
in a bowl until crumbly. Sprinkle half over the crumbled macaroons. Repeat the
layers with the remaining fruit mixture, macaroons and butter mixture. Pour the
liqueur over the top. Bake at 325 degrees for 30 to 40 minutes.

Yield: 20 to 30 servings
BARBARA AND JACK ALAND

Horseradish (Chrain)

1/2 horseradish root

3 tablespoons vinegar

2 to 4 tablespoons water

Pinch of salt

1 small beet, cooked, peeled,

finely chopped

Grate the horseradish in a food processor or by hand. Remove to a bowl. Stir in the vinegar, water and salt. Add enough of the beet to make the horseradish red. Mix well. Pour into a bottle or small jar and cap. Chill until ready to use.

Yield: (about) 2/3 cup

Sandra Vinik

FLOSSIE BAYER'S MATZO DRESSING

$^3/4$ cup chicken fat
$^3/4$ cup finely chopped onion
1 cup chopped celery
1 cup sliced mushrooms
7 cups matzo farfel
2 (10$^1/2$-ounce) cans (or more)
    chicken broth

2 eggs
1 tablespoon paprika
1 teaspoon salt
$^1/2$ teaspoon pepper

Melt the chicken fat in a large skillet. Add the onion, celery and mushrooms and sauté until tender. Add the farfel and sauté until browned. Remove to a large bowl. Add the broth, eggs, paprika, salt and pepper. Stir to mix well. Add additional chicken broth or water if mixture seems dry. Spoon into a well-greased baking dish. Bake at 350 degrees for 35 minutes.

Yield: 12 servings
GAIL BAYER (MRS. JEFFREY)

Lindsay, Gail, Annie, and Jeffrey Bayer

Matzo Farfel Kugels

1 (1-pound) box matzo farfel
2 tablespoons vegetable oil
2 large onions, chopped

7 eggs, beaten
2 teaspoons salt
1/2 teaspoon pepper

Place the farfel in a colander and rinse with cold water; drain well. Heat the oil in a skillet. Add the onions and sauté until translucent. Combine the onions, drained farfel, eggs, salt and pepper in a large bowl. Stir to mix well. Spoon into muffin tins coated with nonstick cooking spray. Bake at 350 degrees for 45 minutes or until golden brown and crispy.

Yield: 12 kugels
LEENIE FOLSOM

PASSOVER SPINACH KUGEL

5 matzo, broken, soaked, drained
1 cup sour cream
4 ounces cream cheese, softened
1 egg, beaten
2 (10-ounce) packages frozen
    chopped spinach, thawed,
    drained

2 tablespoons chopped fresh parsley
2 tablespoons chopped green onion
    tops
Salt and pepper to taste
4 slices Muenster cheese, torn, or
    1/2 cup grated Parmesan cheese

Mix the matzo, sour cream, cream cheese and egg in a bowl. Stir in the spinach, parsley and green onions. Season with salt and pepper. Fold in the Muenster cheese. Pour into a lightly greased baking dish. Bake at 350 degrees for 45 minutes.

Yield: 8 servings
LYNNE AND MARK COHEN

SWEET POTATO AND CARROT TZIMMES

1 cup apple juice
1 cup water
1 (6-ounce) can pineapple juice
2 cups pitted prunes
1 cup dried apricots
1/2 cup golden raisins
2 pounds large carrots, peeled,
    cut into 1/2-inch rounds
2 pounds sweet potatoes, peeled,
    cut into 1/2-inch rounds
Grated zest and juice of 1 lemon

1 tablespoon cinnamon
2 teaspoons grated fresh gingerroot,
    or 1 teaspoon ground ginger
2 teaspoons nutmeg
1/2 cup packed light brown sugar
1/2 cup sugar
Salt and pepper to taste
Sugar, lemon juice or cinnamon
    to taste
Matzo balls, quartered (optional)

Combine the apple juice, water and pineapple juice in a large heavy pot and bring to a boil. Remove from the heat and add the prunes, apricots and raisins. Cover and let stand for 15 minutes. Stir in the carrots, sweet potatoes, lemon zest, lemon juice, cinnamon, gingerroot, nutmeg, brown sugar and sugar. Season with salt and pepper. Bring to a boil over high heat. Reduce the heat to medium. Simmer, covered, for 30 minutes. Uncover and cook for 15 to 30 minutes or until the carrots and sweet potatoes are tender and the sauce is thick and rich. Season with additional sugar, lemon juice or cinnamon. Add the matzo balls. Serve hot or at room temperature.

Yield: 8 to 10 servings
SHERRON GOLDSTEIN

LOUISE LEVIN'S MATZO SHALET

2 (1-pound) boxes matzo farfel
9 eggs
1 1/2 cups sugar
Grated zest and juice of 2 lemons
1 tablespoon cinnamon

1 teaspoon salt
1 cup chicken fat, melted
9 apples, peeled, cored, thinly sliced
2 cups golden raisins

Soak the farfel in water in a bowl for up to 1 hour. Squeeze out all excess water and place the farfel in a large bowl. Beat the eggs and sugar in a bowl with an electric mixer until well blended. Beat in the lemon zest, lemon juice, cinnamon, salt and most of the chicken fat. Add to the farfel. Stir in the apples and raisins and mix well. Spoon into 2 greased 10x16-inch baking pans. Drizzle the remaining chicken fat over the top. Bake at 350 degrees for 1 1/2 hours or until golden brown on top. Cut into squares to serve.

Yield: 16 servings
SUSAN LEVIN SCHLECHTER

Our mother, Louise Levin, was a wonderful cook. From her many recipes I associate with her and her mother Rebecca Aland, is this version of Matzah Shalet, which makes the kitchen smell wonderful on the first night of Passover. Matzah Shalet is a sweet pudding that our mother served as part of the main course of Passover.

Louise Levin, 1945

BUBBE'S PASSOVER ROLLS

1/2 cup peanut oil
1 cup water
1 teaspoon sugar

1 teaspoon salt
2 cups matzo meal
4 eggs

Combine the peanut oil, water, sugar and salt in a saucepan. Bring to a boil. Stir in the matzo meal and remove from the heat. Let cool to room temperature. Beat the eggs in a bowl. Add the cooled matzo mixture and stir to mix well. Let stand for 10 minutes. Shape into 8 to 10 balls and place them about 2 inches apart on a well-greased baking sheet. Bake at 375 degrees for 40 to 50 minutes or until golden brown.

Yield: 8 to 10 rolls

HELEN NAGRODZKI AND LOUISE ABROMS

Levin Family

PASSOVER BAGELS

2/3 cup vegetable oil
1 cup water
Pinch of salt

2 cups matzo meal
6 eggs, beaten

Combine the oil, water and salt in a medium saucepan. Bring to a boil. Remove from the heat and stir in the matzo meal. Return to the heat and cook until thickened, stirring constantly. Remove from the heat and let cool to room temperature. Add the eggs and beat with a fork to mix. Shape the dough into balls and flatten. Place on a greased baking sheet. Push a wet finger in the center of each to make a hole. Bake at 375 degrees for 45 minutes or until puffed and golden brown.

Yield: 10 to 12 bagels
Sarah Halpern

AUNT TESSIE'S PASSOVER MANDEL BRATE

3 eggs
3/4 cup sugar
1/3 cup vegetable oil
3/4 cup matzo meal

3/4 cup chopped almonds
2 tablespoons potato starch
1 teaspoon cinnamon
1/2 teaspoon salt

Beat the eggs, sugar and oil in a bowl. Mix the matzo meal, almonds, potato starch, cinnamon and salt in a bowl. Add to the egg mixture and stir to mix well. Let stand for 10 minutes. Shape into 4 long rolls with oil-coated hands. Add a little matzo meal if the dough is too loose to handle. Place in a greased 10×15-inch baking pan. Bake at 350 degrees for about 40 minutes.

Yield: 12 servings
LYNNE AND MARK COHEN

Aunt Tessie Cohen

Passover was incomplete without Passover goodies from Aunt Tessie's home. Cars would line her driveway, and continue down the street waiting to pick up their Passover orders. Aunt Tessie would invite each person to have a taste of her latest creation all of which were "simply delicious!!" (her words)...and they were! She loved feeding people and loved making people happy. Her granddaughter, Bari Cohen Kuhlman, has preserved Aunt Tessie's recipes.

GRANOLA

2¹/2 cups matzo farfel
1 cup shredded fresh coconut
1 cup coarsely chopped blanched
   almonds
2 to 4 tablespoons margarine

¹/4 cup packed brown sugar
1 tablespoon honey
¹/4 teaspoon salt
¹/2 cup raisins

Mix the farfel, coconut and almonds in a bowl. Spread on a lightly greased baking sheet. Bake at 325 degrees for 15 to 20 minutes or until lightly toasted, stirring several times during baking. Return to the bowl. Combine the margarine, brown sugar, honey and salt in a saucepan. Heat until the margarine melts and the brown sugar dissolves, stirring constantly. Pour over the granola in the bowl and toss to coat well. Spread the granola on the baking sheet. Bake at 300 degrees for 15 minutes or until golden brown, stirring frequently to prevent burning. Remove to a bowl. Add the raisins and toss to mix, breaking apart any clumps. Store in an airtight container when cool.

Yield: (about) 5 cups
RONNE AND DONALD HESS

FARFEL CEREAL

4 cups farfel
1 cup chopped nuts
¹/4 cup vegetable oil

¹/4 cup honey
Raisins to taste

Combine the farfel, nuts, oil and honey in a bowl. Toss until well coated. Spread on a baking sheet. Bake at 350 degrees for 30 minutes, stirring frequently. Remove to a bowl. Add raisins and toss to mix. Store in an airtight container when cool.

Yield: (about) 5 cups
RONNE AND DONALD HESS

ALMOND SPONGE CAKE

7 eggs
1 cup sugar
1 cup White Lily flour

¹/2 cup ground almonds
1 teaspoon almond flavoring

Beat the eggs and sugar in a bowl with an electric mixer until pale yellow. Fold in the flour, almonds and almond flavoring. Pour into a greased 10-inch tube pan. Bake at 350 degrees for 30 minutes or until a wooden pick inserted in the center comes out clean. Remove to a wire rack to cool.

Yield: 10 to 12 servings
KATHERINE HANAN

*Ronne and Donald
Hess Family*

PASSOVER SPONGE CAKE

3/4 cup potato starch
1/4 cup cake flour
9 egg yolks

Pinch of salt
9 egg whites
1 1/2 cups sugar

Sift the potato starch and cake flour into a bowl 5 times. Beat the egg yolks and salt in a bowl until pale yellow. Beat the egg whites in a bowl until foamy. Beat in the sugar gradually and continue beating until stiff and glossy. Fold the egg yolks into the egg white mixture. Fold in the sifted dry ingredients. Pour into an ungreased 10-inch tube pan. Bake at 325 degrees for 1 hour. Invert the pan on a wire rack to cool.

Yield: 10 to 12 servings
SARAH HALPERN

PASSOVER CAKE

¹/2 cup potato starch
¹/2 cup matzo cake meal
12 egg whites
2 cups sugar

12 egg yolks
Grated zest and juice of 1 lemon
Grated zest and juice of 1 orange

Sift the potato starch and cake meal into a bowl 5 times. Beat the egg whites in a bowl until foamy. Beat in the sugar gradually and continue beating until stiff and glossy. Beat the egg yolks in a bowl until pale yellow. Fold the egg yolks into the egg white mixture. Fold in the sifted dry ingredients. Add the grated lemon zest and juice and grated orange zest and juice and fold in gently. Pour into an ungreased 10-inch tube pan. Bake at 350 degrees for 1 hour. Invert the pan on a wire rack to cool.

Yield: 10 to 12 servings
MARION COHEN (MRS. OSCAR)

CHOCOLATE MOUSSE CAKE

1 tablespoon instant coffee crystals
3 tablespoons hot water
3/4 cup (1 1/2 sticks) butter or
    margarine
2 cups semisweet chocolate chips
9 egg yolks

3/4 cup sugar
9 egg whites
1 cup whipping cream
4 ounces chocolate candy bars,
    shaved

Heat the coffee crystals and water in a saucepan, stirring until dissolved. Add the butter and chocolate chips. Cook over low heat until the butter and chocolate melt. Remove to a large bowl and let cool. Beat the egg yolks and sugar in a bowl until thick. Stir into the cooled chocolate mixture. Beat the egg whites in a bowl until stiff. Fold into the chocolate mixture. Pour half the batter into a greased 9-inch springform pan. Bake at 350 degrees for 30 minutes. Remove to a wire rack and let cool to room temperature. Beat the cream in a mixing bowl and fold into the remaining batter. Pour on top of the cooled cake. Sprinkle with the shaved chocolate. Cover and freeze until firm. Remove from the freezer 20 minutes before serving.

Note: The butter and chocolate can be melted in a microwave-safe bowl in the microwave.

Yield: 8 to 10 servings
BARBARA AND JACK ALAND

PASSOVER FARFEL COOKIES

2 cups matzo meal
2 cups farfel
1 1/2 cups sugar
1 cup raisins, chopped nuts or
    a combination

1 teaspoon cinnamon
2/3 cup vegetable oil
5 eggs

Mix the matzo meal, farfel, sugar, raisins and cinnamon in a bowl. Add the oil and eggs and beat until well mixed. Shape the dough with oiled hands into 1-inch balls. Place on greased baking sheets, 12 balls per sheet. Press to flatten slightly. Bake at 350 degrees for 25 minutes. Remove immediately to a wire rack to cool.

Yield: 3 1/2 to 4 dozen cookies
AVIE COHEN

PASSOVER BROWNIES

4 eggs
2 cups sugar
1/2 cup baking cocoa
1 cup vegetable oil

1/2 teaspoon salt
1 cup matzo cake meal, sifted
1 cup chopped nuts
2 cups semisweet chocolate chips

Beat the eggs well in a bowl. Add the sugar and beat until light and fluffy. Stir in the baking cocoa, oil and salt. Stir in the cake meal gradually. Add the nuts and chocolate chips and stir to mix well. Pour into a greased 9x13-inch baking pan. Bake at 325 degrees for 30 minutes or until the brownies pull away from the sides of the pan. Remove to a wire rack to cool.

Yield: 2 dozen brownies
BARBARA ALAND

I got this recipe from my sister, Betsy. She wasn't home when I needed it the first time so my brother-in-law read it to me. He said 1 box of matzo cake meal instead of 1 cup! Boy, were they bricks!

PASSOVER TOFFEE

3¹/₃ matzos
¹/₂ cup (1 stick) butter
¹/₂ cup (1 stick) margarine

1 cup packed brown sugar
2 cups semisweet chocolate chips
12 ounces chopped nuts (optional)

Line a 10×15-inch baking pan with foil. Arrange the matzos on the foil to cover the bottom of the pan. Combine the butter, margarine and brown sugar in a saucepan. Bring to a boil, stirring constantly. Cook for 3 minutes. Pour over the matzos and spread evenly. Bake at 425 degrees for 5 minutes. Remove from the oven and sprinkle with the chocolate chips. Let stand for a few minutes for the chocolate to soften. Spread the chocolate evenly over the toffee layer. Sprinkle with the nuts. Chill until firm and break into pieces.

Yield: 24 to 36 pieces
Sarah Ellen Levine and Marissa Apolinsky

IMBERLACH

This is a Passover candy with a ginger flavor.

6 cups grated carrots
3¹/₂ cups sugar
Grated zest and juice of 2 oranges,
    or 1 tablespoon frozen orange
    juice concentrate

Juice of ¹/₂ lemon
1¹/₂ teaspoons ginger
¹/₂ cup walnuts

Combine the carrots and sugar in a saucepan and bring to a boil. Cook at a rapid boil, stirring often, for about 1 hour or until the mixture pulls away from the side of the pan and holds its shape when a small amount is spooned onto a plate. Remove from the heat and stir in the orange zest, orange juice, lemon juice, ginger and walnuts. Pour onto a wet pastry board. Spread the mixture to a ¹/₂-inch-thick slab. Let stand overnight. Cut into diamond shapes.

Yield: about 12 dozen candies
Sandra Vinik

HOMEMADE SOAP SHAPES

Here's an idea for an excellent gift for children to make. I made these with my 4½-year-old and 20-month-old for Hanukkah and they had lots of fun. We made dreidels and Stars of David using cookie cutters and blue food coloring.

2 bars white soap
2 tablespoons white hand lotion

Food coloring

Grate the soap into a gallon-size sealable plastic bag. Add the lotion and food coloring to achieve desired shade. Seal the bag and squeeze to mix. Remove the soap from the bag and form into a ball. Place on a work surface and flatten to ½ inch thick. Cut with cookie cutters and place on a wire rack to dry for a few days.

KATIE ICIMSOY

CONTRIBUTORS

Barbara Abrams
Judy Abroms
Louise Abroms
Barbara and Jack
　Aland
Karen Allen
Linda Applebaum
Bernice Barstein
Susan Barstein
Gail and Jeffrey
　Bayer
Harry Bayer
Joan Becker
Nancy Berland
Barbara Betten
Susan K. Biedinger
Jann Blitz
Jane Bluestein
Peggy Bonfield
Judy Borisky
Leona Cherner
Harriet Cogan
Avie Cohen
Justin Cohen
Lois Cohen
Lynne and Mark
　Cohen
Marion Cohen
Norman Cohen
Patsy Collat
　(Mrs. Charles, Sr.)
Phoebe M. Cotton
Frances Cypress
Nancy Denney
Dian Diamond
Ellen Dorsky
Lori Dorsky
Sallie Datnoff Downs
Dr. Rick Elkus
Ellen Elsas
Gladys Epstein

Kaydee Erdreich-
　Bremen
Estelle Eubanks
Chu-Chi Fierman
Johanna "JoJo"
　Levenson
　Fitzpatrick
Celeste Fleisher
Ethel Fleisher
Leenie Folsom
Cathy O. Friedman
Faye Friedman
Esther Glick
Fran Godchaux
Nancy Goedecke
Donna Goldberg
Betty Goldstein
Hannah Goldstein
Sally Goldstein
Sherron Goldstein
Joanna Gotlieb
Mollie Gotlieb
　(Mrs. Herman)
Rosalie Gotlieb
Ida Grafman
　(Mrs. Milton)
Jeanne Hagedorn
Sarah Halpern
Katherine Hanan
Natalie Hausman-
　Weiss
Cissy Held
Ginger Held
Joyce Helzberg
Carol Herman
Gail Herman
Jimmie Hess
Ronne and Donald
　Hess
Mackie Horowitz
Gloria Howton

Katie Icimsoy
Bella Imas
Ilene Rosenfeld
　Johnson
Adeline Kahn
Frederick Kaimann
Rhoda Kaplan
Elaine Kartus
Irma Koch
Rochelle Koslin
Allyn Holladay
　Krall
Shirley Leader
Marion Leaf
Sonya Lefkovits
Gayle Leitman
Faye Levin
Sarah Ellen Levine
Julie Levinson-Gabis
Denise Lewis
Lee Unger Lichter
Betty Loeb
Judy Luks
Kate Malkove
Letty Marcus
Julie Marks
Margot Marx
Laurie Max
Anita May
Jocelyn McClelland-
　Tandet
Candy Meyerson
Anne Michelson
Ann Mollengarden
Cathy Moore
Barbara Bersch
　Newman
Jamie and Greg
　Odrezin
Babs Perlman
Lauren Perlman

Lenore Picard
Carrie Pizitz
Loraine Reznik
Kim Rosemore
Cantor Jessica
　Roskin
Bunny and Joel
　Rotenstreich
Jenifer Rotenstreich
Judy Rotenstreich
Kim Roth
Kit Roth
Judy C. Rutstein
Amy Saag
Sharon Samen
Pat Saul
Judi Schulman-Miller
Ferne Seigel
Jane Seigel
Sandra Shulman
Rosalyn Siegal
Anne Silberman
Carole Simpson
Jean Sklar
Betty Steinmetz
Ceil Sundock
Marilyn Tanner
Debby Thomas
George Thompson
Sandra Vinik
Jackie Waites
Norma Warren
Julie Watson
Allison Weil
Lori Weil
Pat Weil
Barbara Weisberg

INDEX